JOE PORCARO'S GROOVIN' WITH THE Odd Times

PATTERNS FOR ROCK, JAZZ, AND LATIN AT THE DRUMSET

by Joe Porcaro

ISBN 978-1-4234-6852-3

7777 W. BLUEMOUND RD. P.O. BOX 13819 MILWAUKEE, WI 53213

In Australia Contact:
Hal Leonard Australia Pty. Ltd.
4 Lentara Court
Cheltenham, Victoria, 3192 Australia
Email: ausadmin@halleonard.com.au

Visit Hal Leonard Online at
www.halleonard.com

This book is dedicated to my son Jeff Porcaro, who showed us so much in so little time.

Preface

Many of today's composers and musical groups are searching for new approaches in their music; one of these being the asymmetric meters (odd times). Therefore, I feel there is a great need for a guide to the odd times in jazz, Latin, and rock.

These ideas were developed through my experiences with composers and artists such as Emil Richards, Lalo Schifrin, Dave Grusin, Roger Kellaway, Tom Scott, Oliver Nelson, Don Ellis, Dave Mackay, and Ralph Humphrey.

Thanks to the following people who have influenced my drumming: Ed Roccetti, Gary Ferguson, Mike Snyder, Ralph Humphrey, Tony Inzalaco, Max Roach, Philly Joe Jones, Steve Schaffer, and John Guerin.

This manual is also dedicated to my wife and to my family: Jeff, Joleen, Mike, and Steve. Special thanks to my grandson, Chase Duddy, who recorded the examples.

Joe Porcaro plays DW drums, Zildjian cymbals, Vic Firth Diamond Tip drum sticks, Beato drum bags, and Aquarian drumheads.

Happy drumming.

Joe Porcaro

Contents

About the Author

Originally from Hartford, Connecticut, drummer and percussionist Joe Porcaro was a natural musician who began marching with his dad as a child. He has recorded on drums and percussion with some of the most recognizable names in the jazz world: Stan Getz, Gerry Mulligan, Freddie Hubbard, Don Ellis, and Mike Manieri.

He may be primarily known as a jazz drummer extraordinaire, but Joe has also played percussion with a wide variety of artists, including Frank Sinatra, Sarah Vaughn, Luciano Pavarotti, Natalie Cole, and Madonna.

His work can be heard on numerous feature film scores and television shows performing with a variety of composers such as Danny Elfman, James Horner, James Newton Howard, John Williams, and Jerry Goldsmith.

Known for his broad range of musical capabilities, Joe passed his love and talent for music on to his sons, Steve, Mike, and Jeff, all of whom created their own successful music careers.

Steve is a keyboardist and composer, and Mike plays bass and cello. Before his untimely death in 1992, Jeff, like his dad both a drummer and percussionist, co-founded the band Toto, which allowed all three brothers to work together and included Joe on the GRAMMY award®-winning album, *Toto IV*.

Joe also loves passing his knowledge on to students at the Los Angeles Music Academy (LAMA) in Pasadena, California, where he is co-chair of the drum department along with Ralph Humphrey. LAMA is a school that focuses on guitar, drumming, bass, and vocals.

Joe is part of the teaching staff on the Drum Channel along with Dom Lombardi and Ralph Humphrey.

Drumset Legend

In this guide to odd times, the student may encounter some rhythmic variations in the 7/4 and 7/8 examples. It was done intentionally to show other variations.

The stress sign (–) is applied under certain notes to help you get the proper feel between cymbal, snare drum, and bass drum.

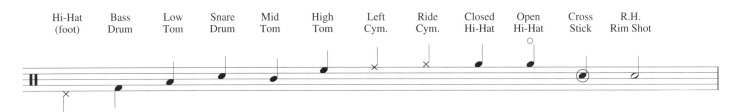

Make sure to count aloud when practicing the exercises. The counting is written in for each group of exercises for the benefit of the student.

PART 1
Jazz Cymbal Patterns in 7/4 and 7/8

Section 1

In the following exercises, the cymbal patterns will be played in even quarters and eights, in groups of two and three. They should be practiced with the right hand only on the ride cymbal. When the counting and feel of them is mastered, the counting should eventually be left out.

The exercises will be shown in 7/4 and 7/8. The tempo for the 7/4 and 7/8 exercises should be the same. The reason for this is that some of the practical application exercises become involved rhythmically and will be easier to read in 7/4 than in 7/8.

Even quarters and eights are to be played in the following exercises. Do not play triplets in the groups of three. The student may count in groups of three and two: 3+2+2 (123–12–12), 2+2+3 (12–12–123), 2+3+2 (12–123–12).

− = the note is stressed

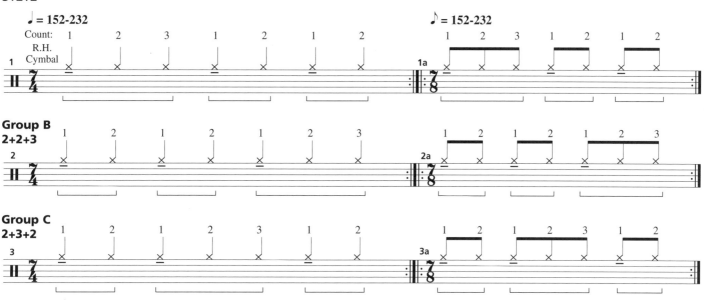

Section 2

In ensemble application, the phrasing of the melody will determine which grouping is to be applied. In the following examples, when playing the bass drum and stressing the first note of each grouping, the student will feel these patterns a little easier. The counting of the three's and two's is shown. The tempo in 7/8 should be the same as 7/4. Observe hi-hat application.

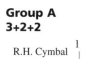
Track 1

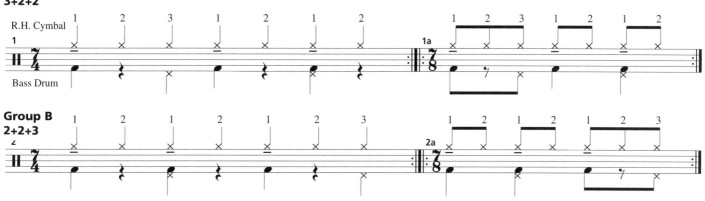

Group C
2+3+2

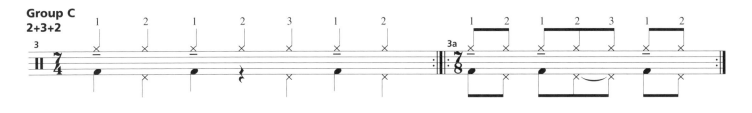

Section 3

Basic Practical Application of the Previous Exercises to the Drumset

Track 2

Basic Pattern Group A
3+2+2

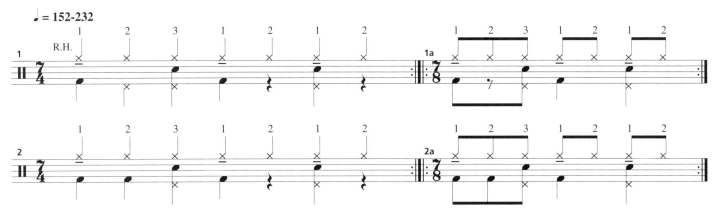

Basic Pattern Group B
2+2+3

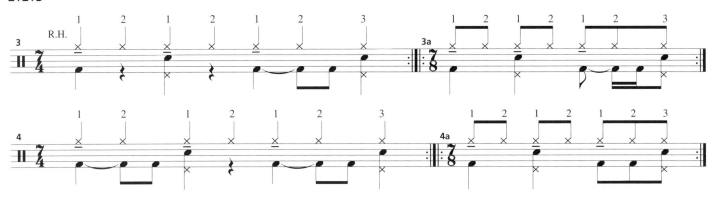

Basic Pattern Group C
2+3+2

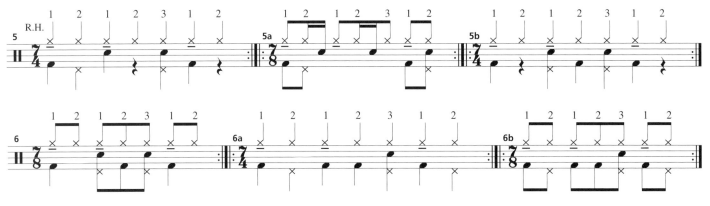

PART 2
Explanation of Snare and Bass Drum Combinations

Section 1

Preparatory Exercises

In the following examples, time keeping in 2/4 and 3/4 is eighth-note triplets. In 2/8 and 3/8, time keeping is sixteenth-note triplets. The snare and bass drum are played while keeping time. Avoid playing flams when the snare or bass are played at the same time as the cymbal.

Track 3

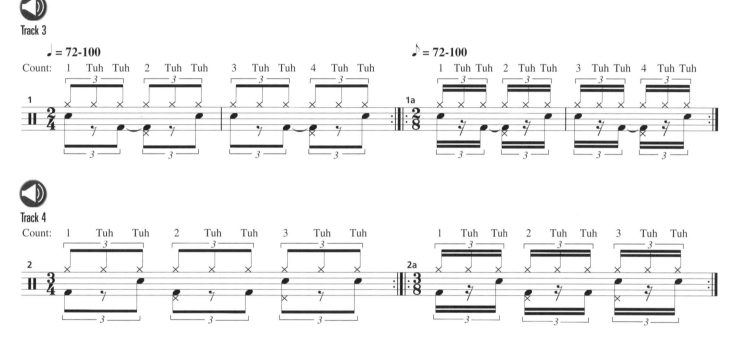

When the student masters the previous exercises, count the number only and leave out the Tuh Tuh's.

Section 2

Snare and Bass Drum Combinations in 2/4 and 2/8 Time

While keeping time with the cymbal, apply the following snare and bass drum combinations. Count eighth or sixteenth note triplets out loud.

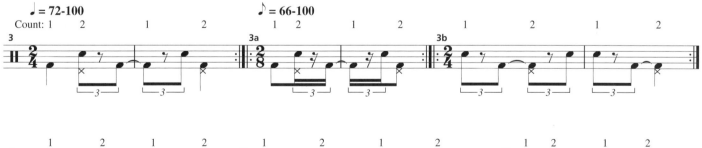

Section 3

Preparatory Exercises

Snare and Bass Drum Combinations in 3/4 and 3/8 Time

Apply 3/4 and 3/8 triplet time keeping while applying the following snare and bass drum combinations.

Count triplets out loud.

Track 5

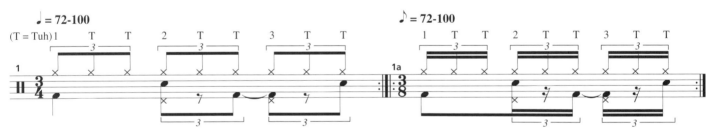

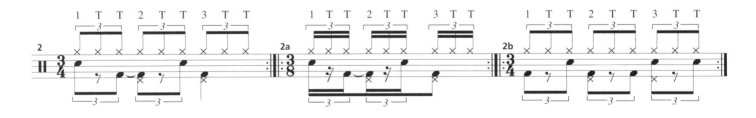

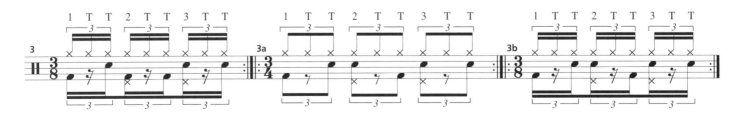

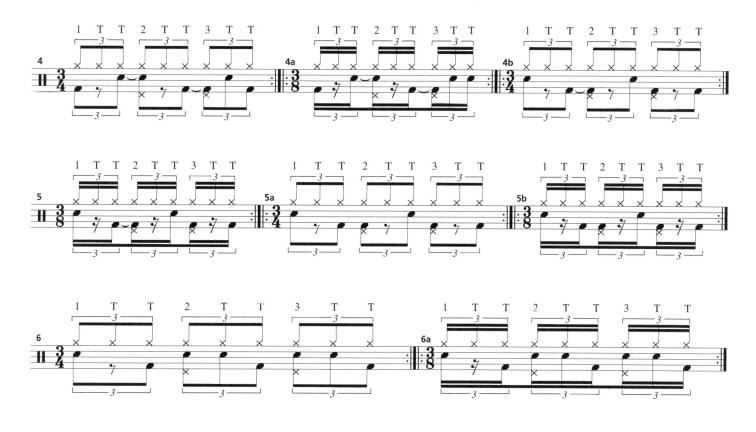

Be creative with the hi-hat in the groupings of three.

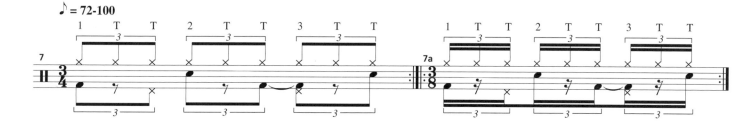

Track 6

♪ = 72-100

PART 3
Practical Application to the Drumset in 7/4 and 7/8

Section 1

Some of the following examples can be applied as time grooves and others can be applied to punctuate two- and four-bar phrases. Combine the first example in line one as a time-groove with the first example in line three to punctuate the two-bar phrase. In section one (3+2+2), counting is 1 2 3–1 2–1 2. Note: In the following pages be aware that some of the 7/4 and 7/8 examples are not rhythmically the same.

Track 7

Group A
3+2+2

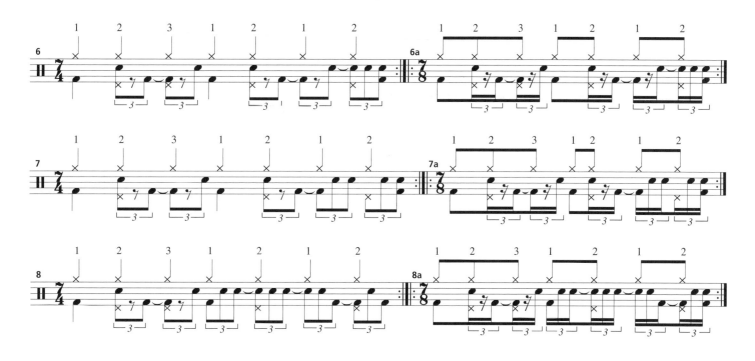

Section 2

At this point the student should be familiar with the notations in 7/8. The following exercises are written in 7/8 only. If at this point the student is not secure with the notations in 7/8, he can transcribe them into 7/4. In section 2, the counting is 1 2–1 2–1 2 3 (2+2+3).

Track 8

♪ = 152-208

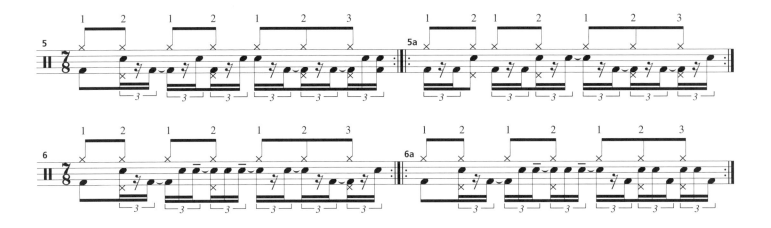

Section 3

Counting is 1 2–1 2 3–1 2 (2+3+2).

PART 4
Developing Jazz Cymbal Time in 7/8

In the following section we will substitute for the groups of two and three, the jazz cymbal phrasing. These are to be played with the right hand for right-handed drummers, or left hand for left-handed drummers. Make sure to count out loud when practicing.

Examples of Two's in 2/4

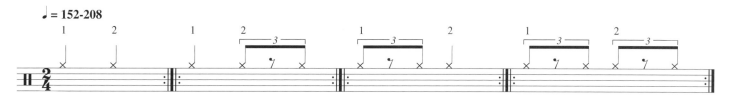

Examples of Two's in 2/8

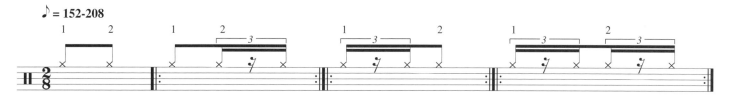

Examples of Three's in 3/4

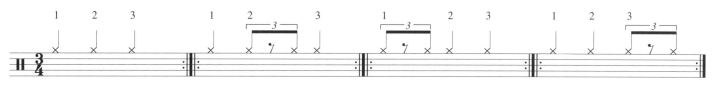

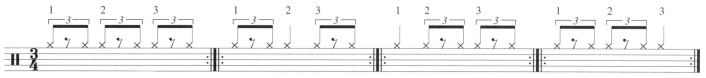

Examples of Three's in 3/8

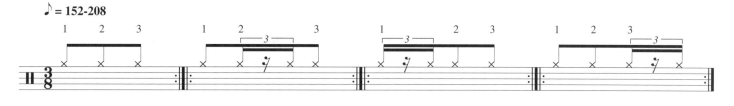

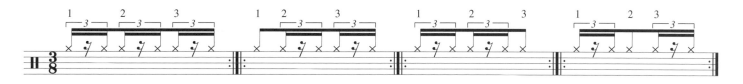

PART 5
Vocabulary of Jazz Cymbal Time Variations

Section 1

The following section will be notated in 7/8 only. The examples should be practiced with the right or left hand and from medium to very fast tempos. Observe the bass drum and hi-hat application. Apply them on all examples. Section one counting is 1 2 3–1 2–1 2 (3+2+2).

Track 10

Group A
3+2+2

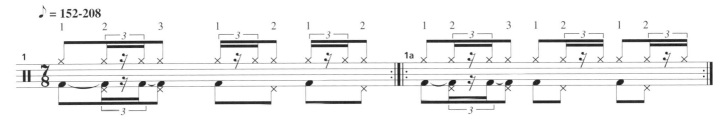

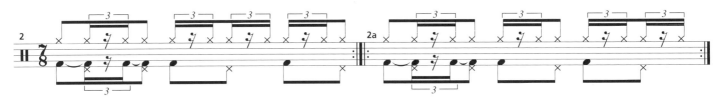

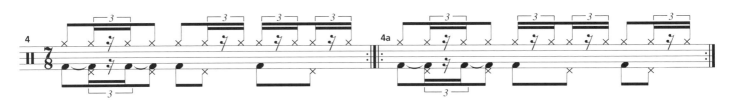

Group B
3+2+2

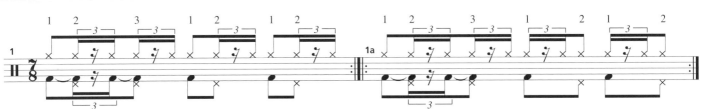

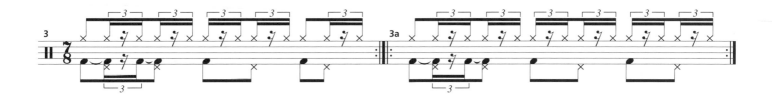

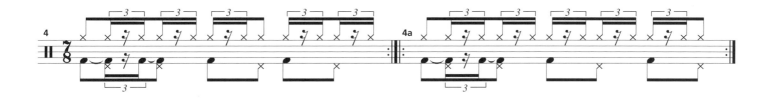

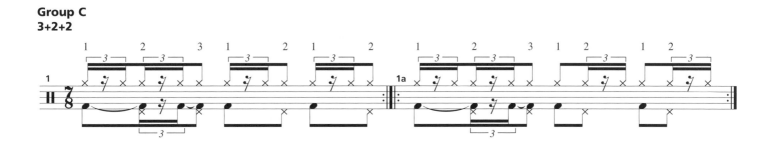

Group C
3+2+2

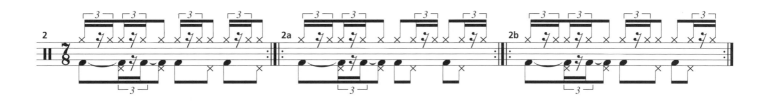

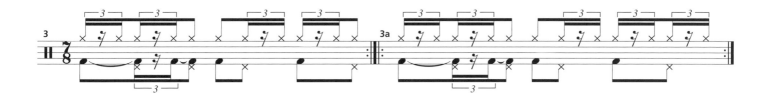

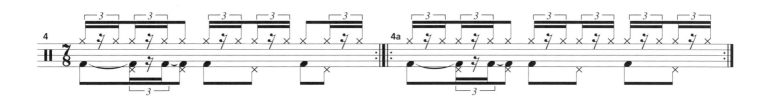

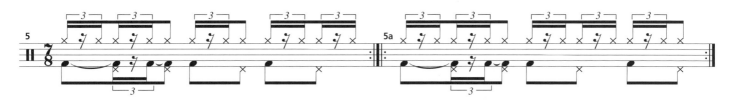

Group D
3+2+2

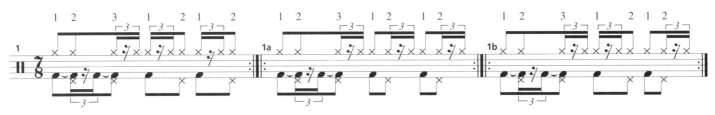

Group E
3+2+2

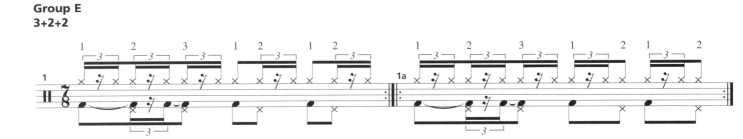

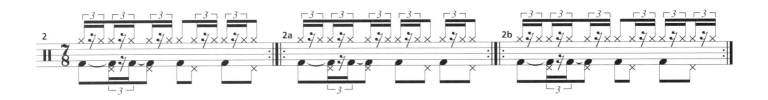

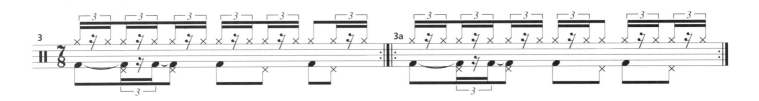

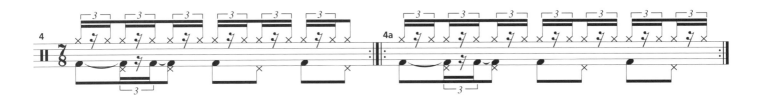

Group F
3+2+2

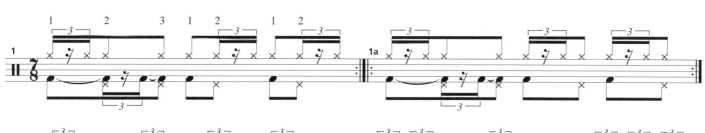

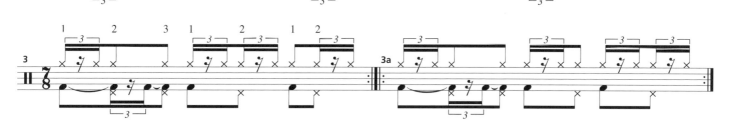

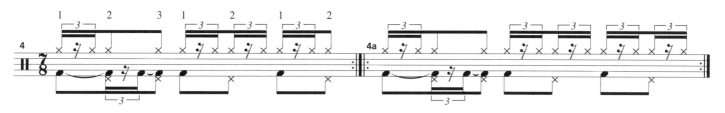

Group G
3+2+2

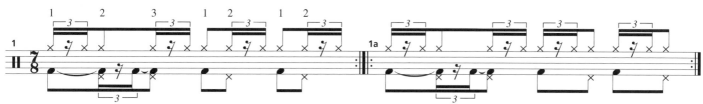

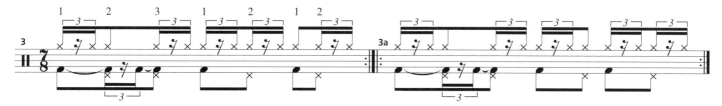

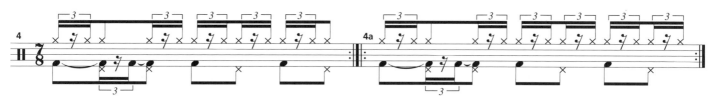

Section 2

Counting is 1 2–1 2–1 2 3 (2+2+3)

Track 11

Group A
2+2+3

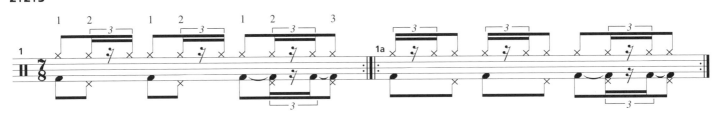

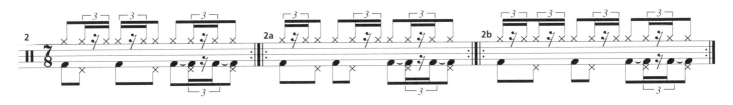

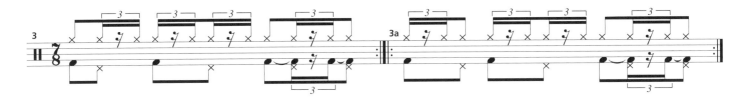

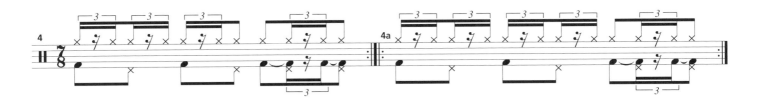

Group B
2+2+3

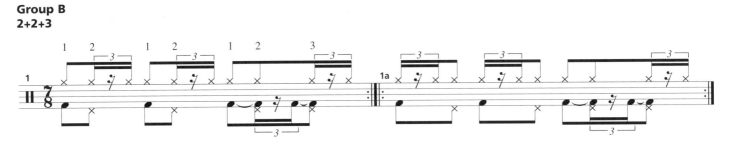

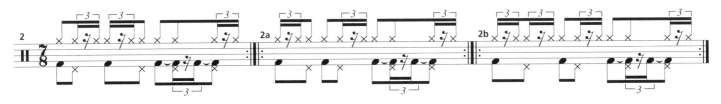

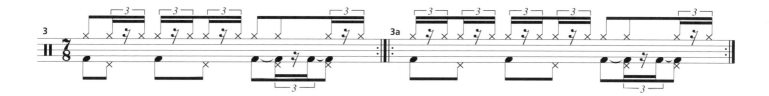

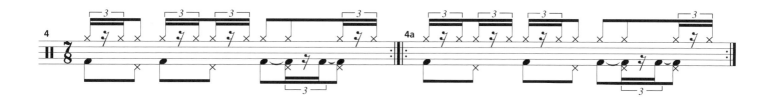

Group C
2+2+3

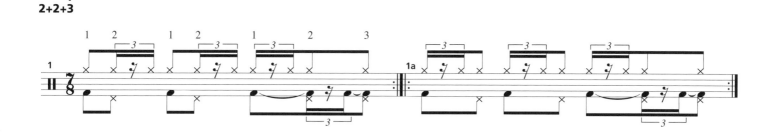

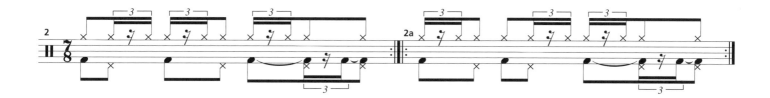

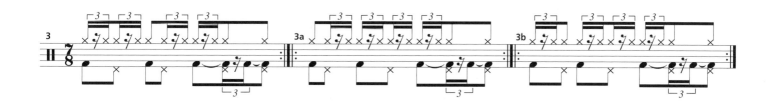

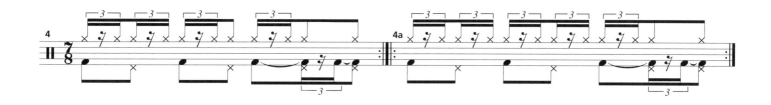

Group D
2+2+3

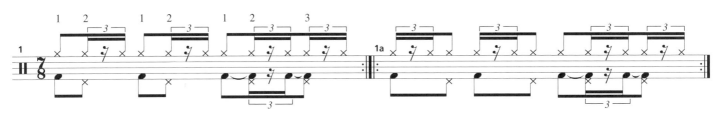

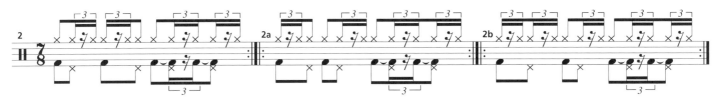

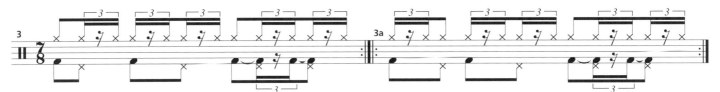

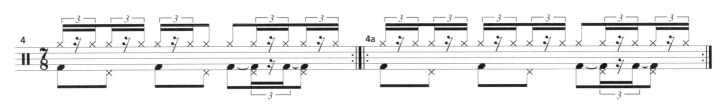

Group E
2+2+3

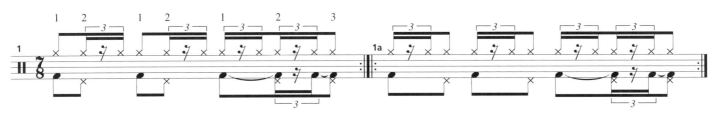

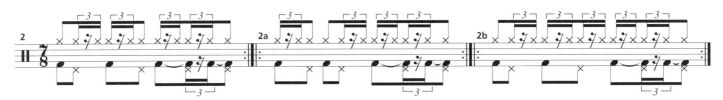

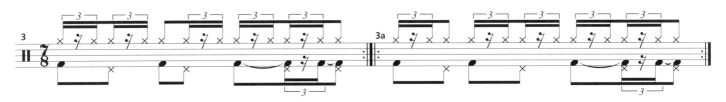

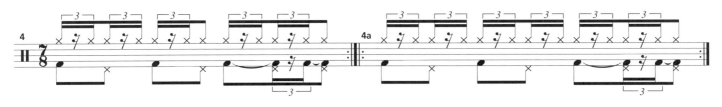

Group F
2+2+3

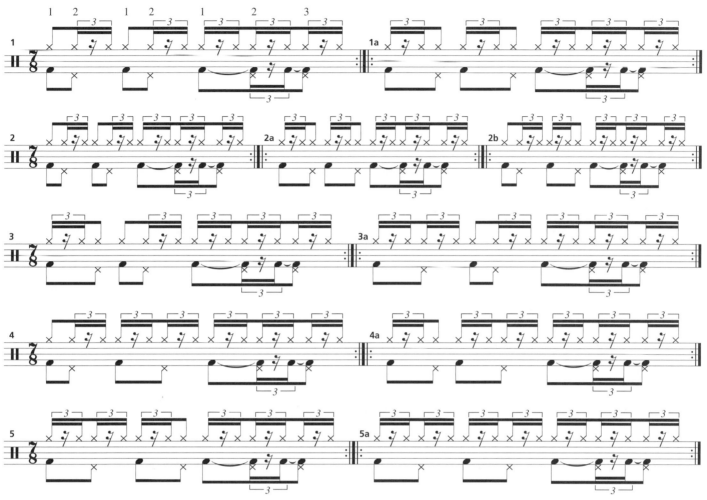

Group G
2+2+3

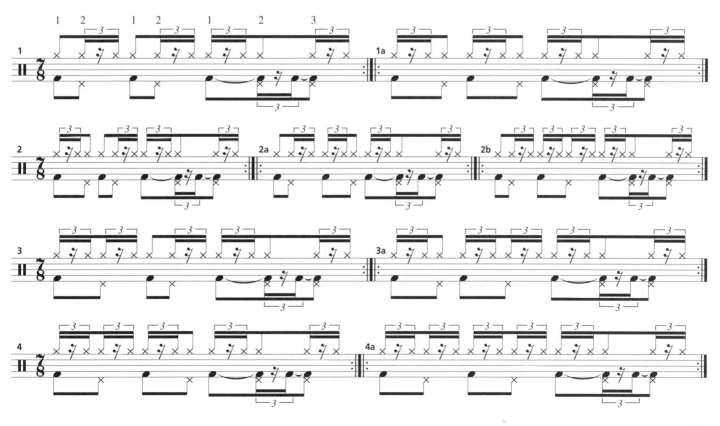

Section 3

Counting is 1 2–1 2 3–1 2 (2+3+2).

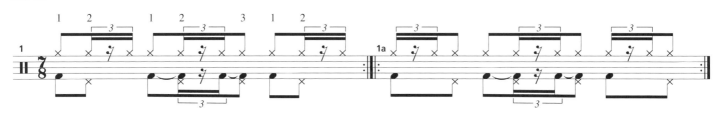

Track 12

Group A
2+3+2

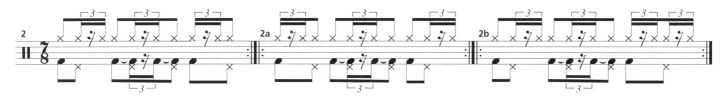

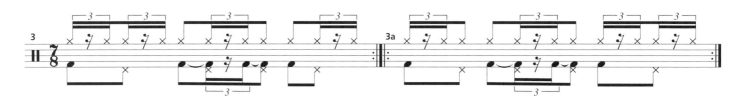

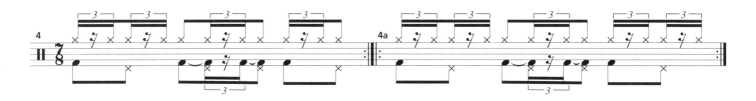

Group B
2+3+2

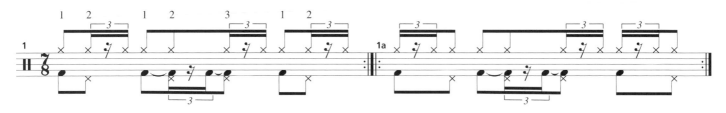

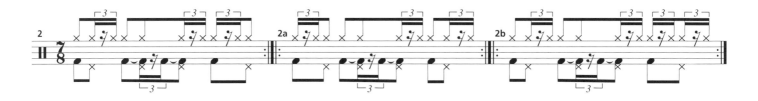

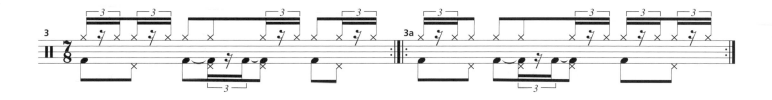

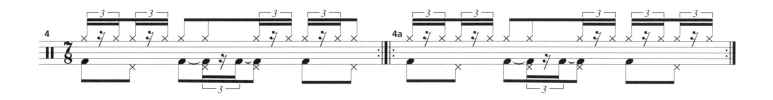

Group C
2+3+2

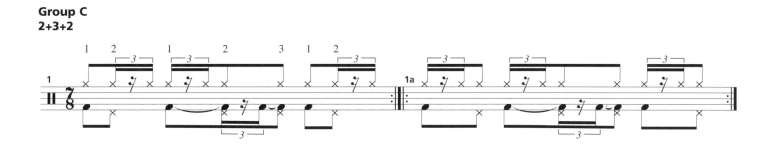

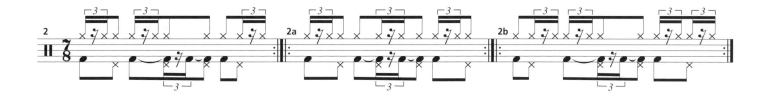

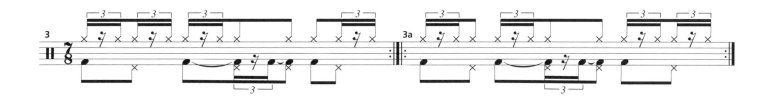

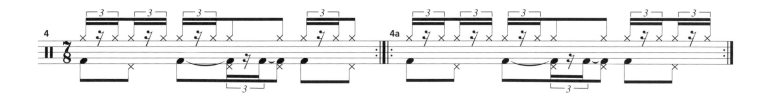

Group D
2+3+2

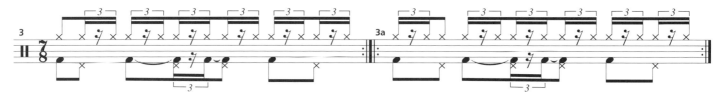

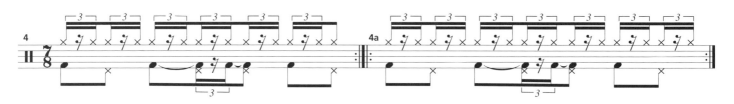

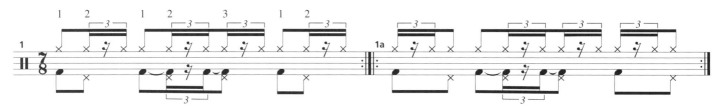

Group E
2+3+2

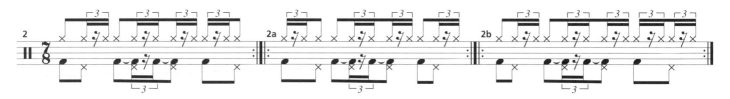

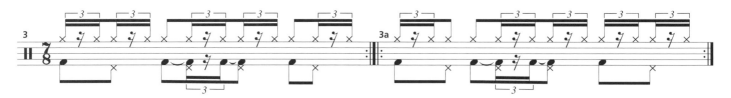

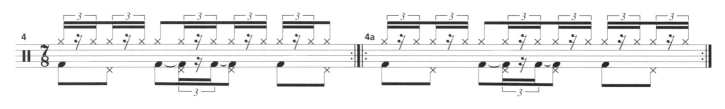

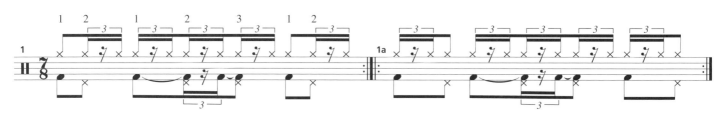

Group F
2+3+2

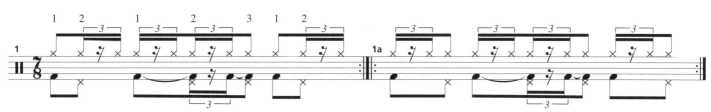

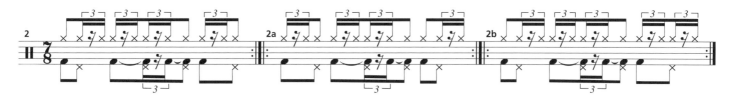

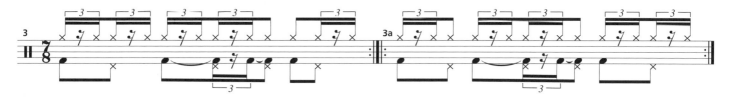

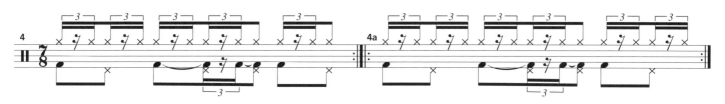

Group G
2+3+2

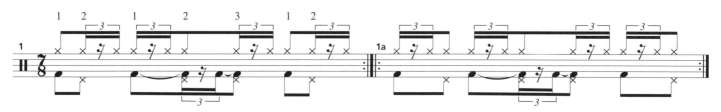

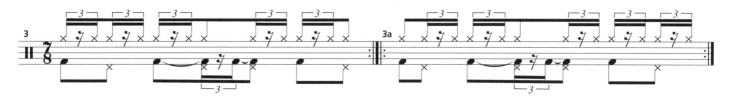

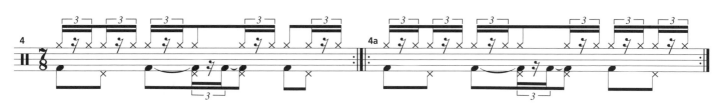

PART 6
Application of the Previous Exercises to the Drumset

Section 1

If the patterns in 7/8 become too involved rhythmically, the student should transcribe them into 7/4. The tempo in 7/4 is the same as in 7/8. Observe the hi-hat.

Track 13

Group A
3+2+2

Counting: 1 2 3–1 2–1 2

Track 14

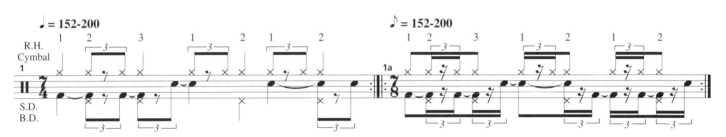

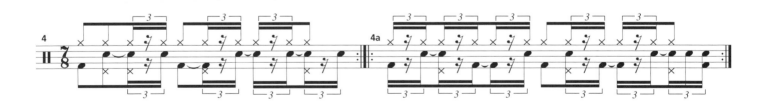

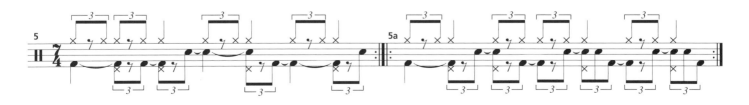

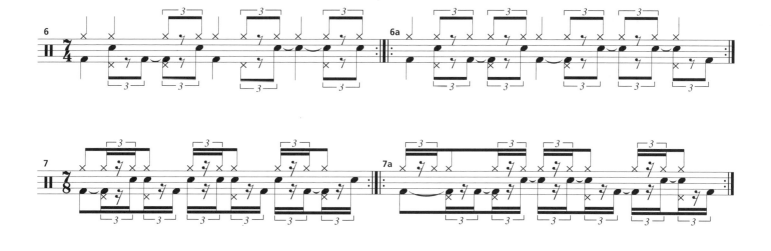

Section 2

Track 15

Group B
2+2+3

Counting is 1 2–1 2–1 2 3.

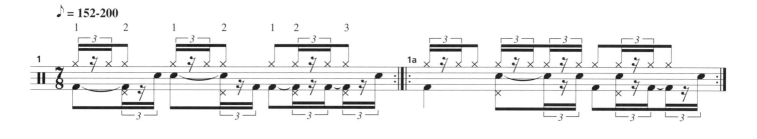

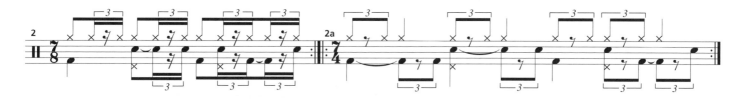

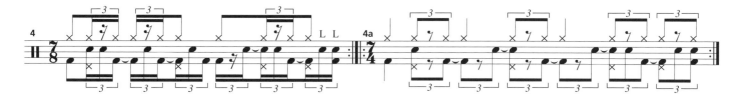

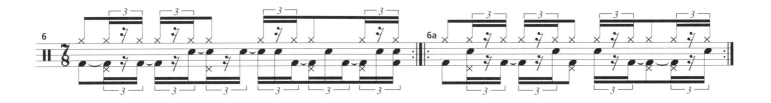

Section 3

Track 16

Group C
2+3+2

Counting is 1 2–1 2 3–1 2.

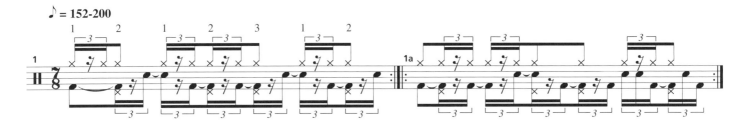

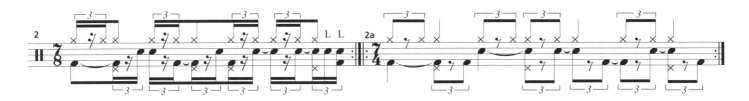

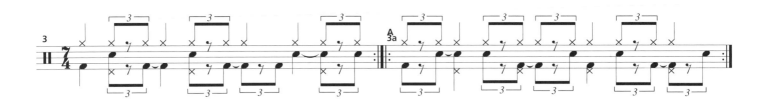

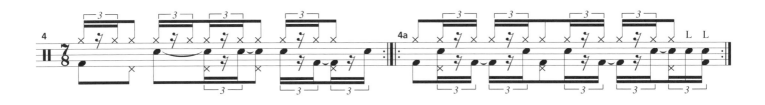

PART 7
Time-Keeping Variations in 7/8

By combining the jazz phrasing of the three's and two's with the even eights of the groups of three and two, we can develop rhythmical variations. There are many variations of these patterns. Students should take it upon themselves to invent some of their own patterns. These patterns are effective for very fast tempos.

Group A counting is 1 2 3–1 2–1 2 (3+2+2).

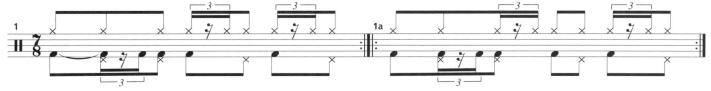

Group B counting is 1 2–1 2–1 2 3 (2+2+3).

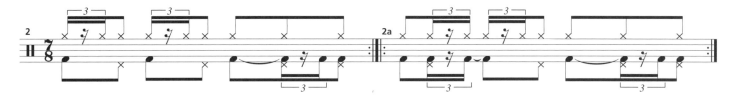

Group C counting is 1 2–1 2 3–1 2 (2+3+2).

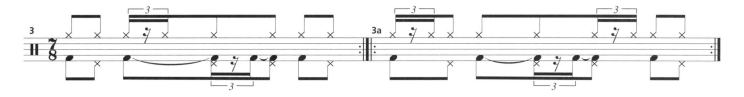

PART 8
Applying Tied Notes to Cymbal Patterns

Section 1

By applying tied notes to the cymbal patterns, we can develop a vocabulary of cymbal grooves.

Example in 3/4

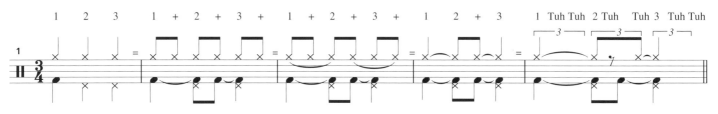

The sound of this rhythm is sometimes called splitting the three in half, and theoretically called a duple rhythm. You're playing two even pulses against three pulses.

Rhythmic Notations

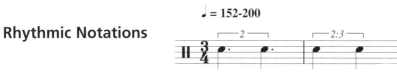

Example in 3/8

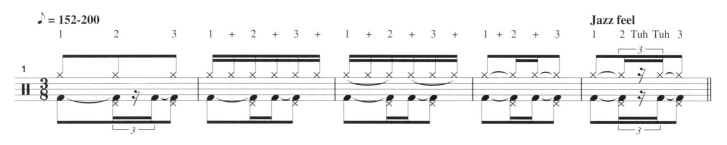

Rhythmic Notations

Section 2

Application

With the use of the new variation of the group of three, we get some interesting cymbal patterns for time keeping. Count out loud with each example when practicing.

Group A
3+2+2

Group B
2+2+3

Group C
2+3+2

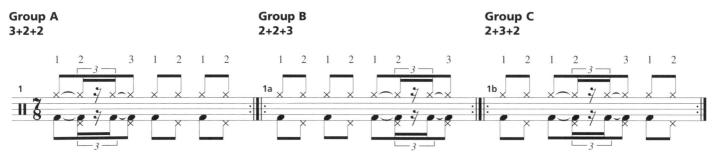

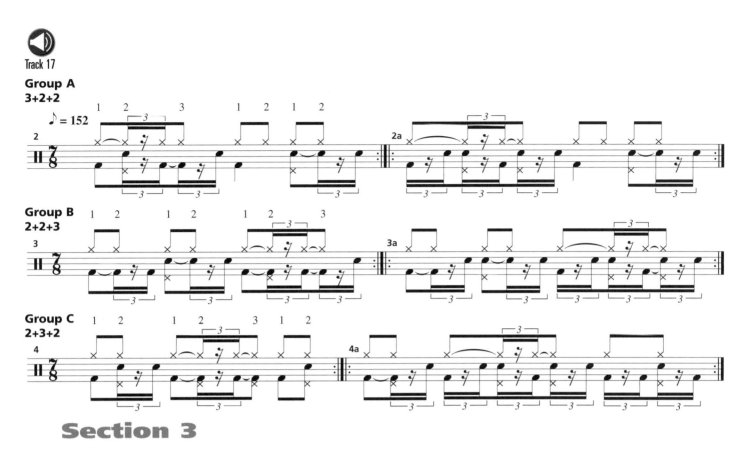

Group A
3+2+2

Group B
2+2+3

Group C
2+3+2

Section 3

Many variations can be applied by the use of the tie, in the groups of three and two. Remember to count out loud. Use the first measure of example 1 as a check pattern throughout the exercises in this group.

Count the two-bar phrase out loud.

Group A
Groups of Three

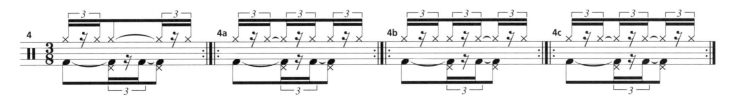

Use the first measure as a check pattern throughout the exercises in this group. Play hi-hat on 2 and 4 throughout this section.

Group B
Groups of Two

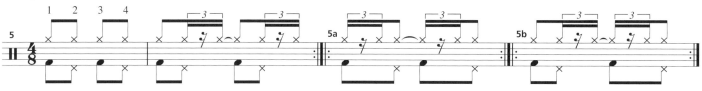

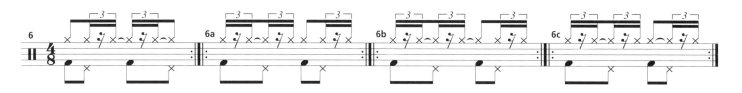

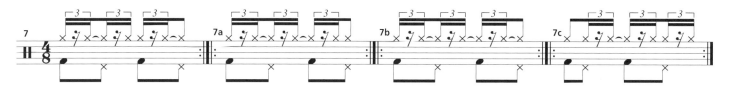

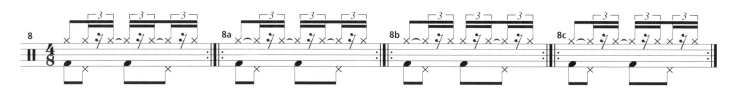

Section 4

By combining the groups of three and two with tied notes, we can get many variations of the jazz cymbal patterns. Some of the possibilities will be shown. Students should take it upon themselves to make up some of their own patterns. Remember to count out loud while practicing.

Group A
3+2+2

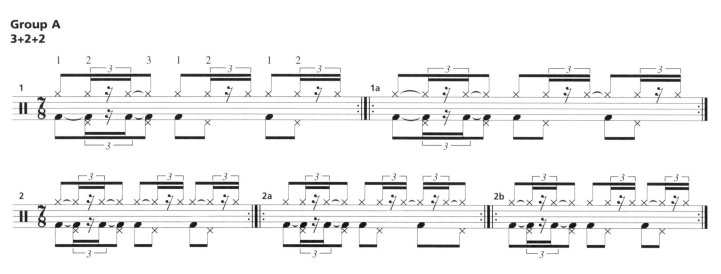

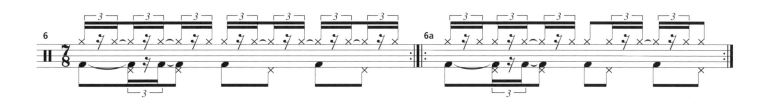

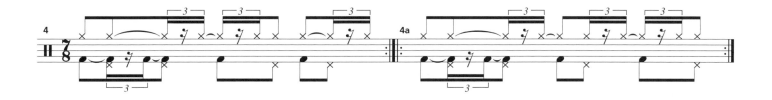

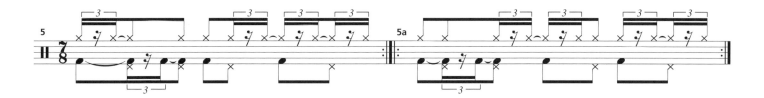

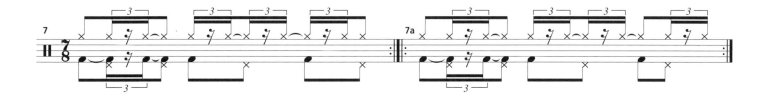

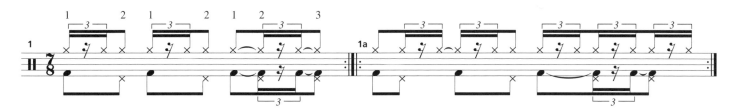

Section 5

Group B
2+2+3

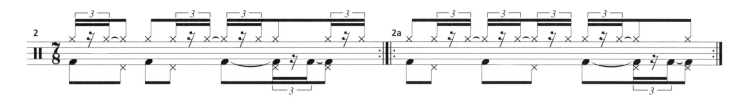

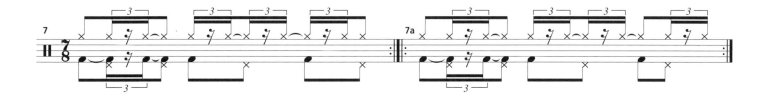

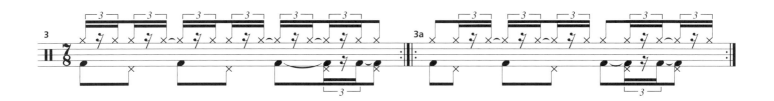

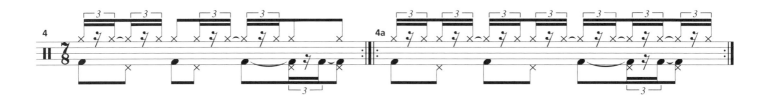

Section 6

Group C
2+3+2

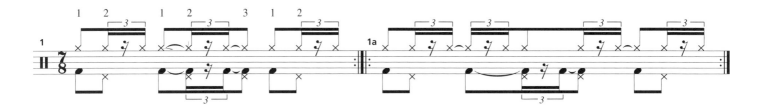

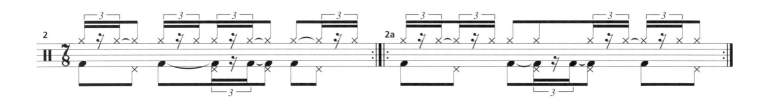

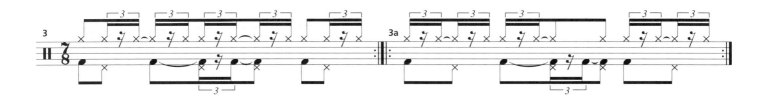

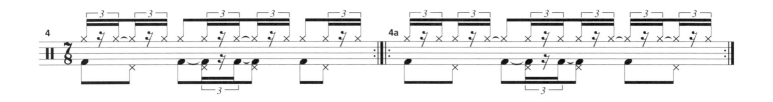

Section 7

Practical Application of the Tied Cymbal Patterns to the Drumset

The following examples can be applied as turnarounds to punctuate four-bar phrases. In the following section the exercises will be shown in 7/8 only. If the exercises become difficult to play, they should be transcribed into 7/4 for easier notation reading.

Track 18

Group A
3+2+2

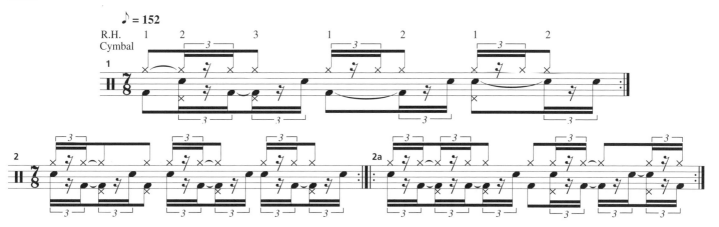

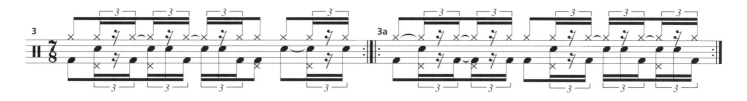

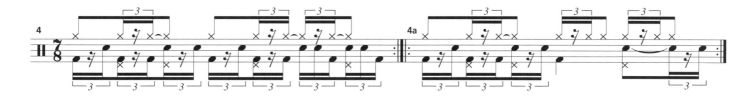

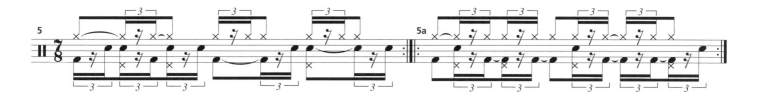

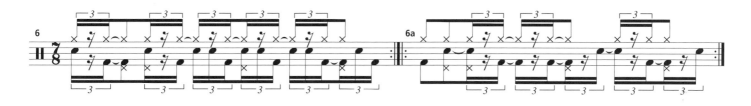

Section 8

Track 19

Group B
2+2+3

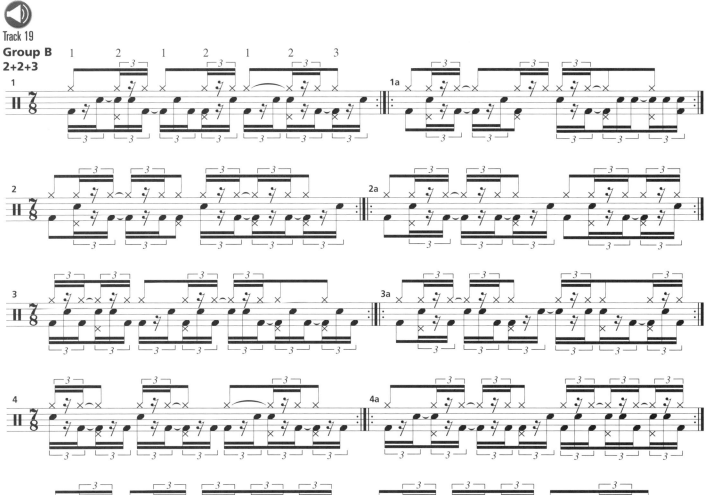

Section 9

Track 20

♪ = 152-200

Group C
2+3+2

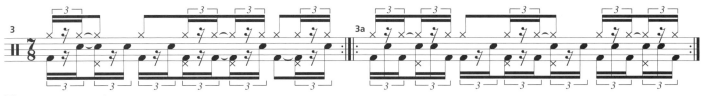

Section 10

Interesting patterns for drum fills can be developed by taking the rhythms of the jazz cymbal beats and orchestrating them on different drums and cymbals of the drumset. Left-handed drummers should reverse the stickings shown.

Track 21

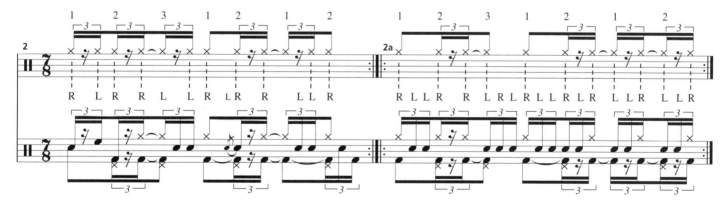

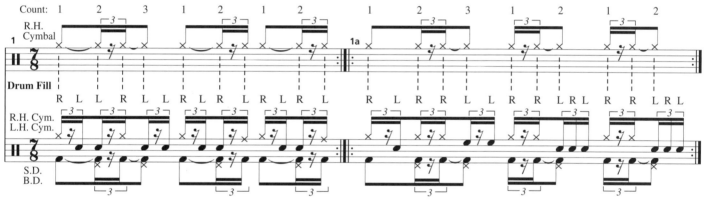

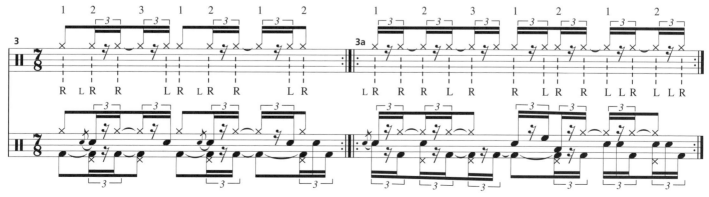

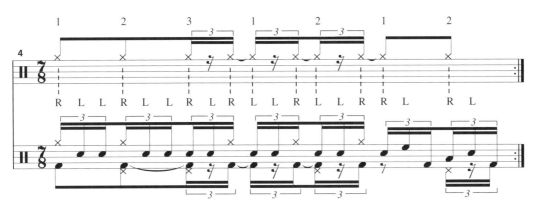

At this point students should take it upon themselves to compose their own time-keeping patterns and fills in 7/8 with the groupings of 2-2-3, 3-2-2, 2-3-2.

Section 11

The following patterns will be in two-bar phrases. The two-bar patterns can be used to punctuate cadences of compositions of four- and eight-bar phrases. The two-bar phrase will also give us opportunity to utilize other groupings. These groupings will also give an over-the-bar feeling in 7/8.

Group A
3+3+3+3+2 (9/8 + 5/8)

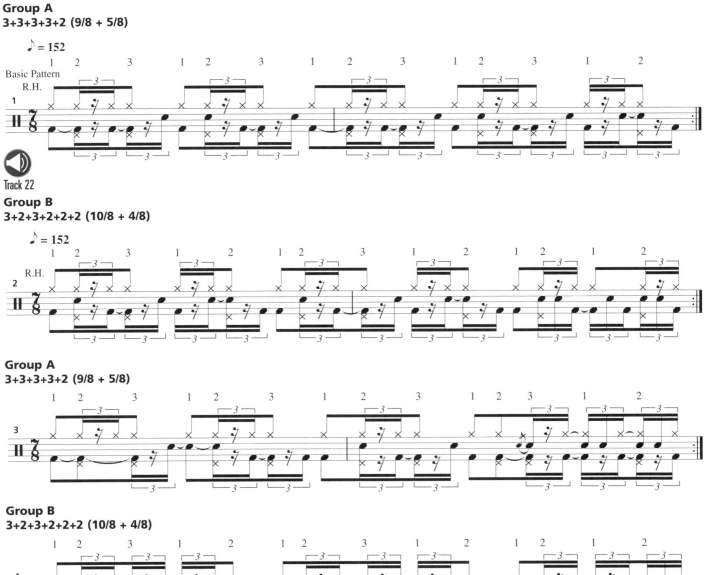

Track 22

Group B
3+2+3+2+2+2 (10/8 + 4/8)

Group A
3+3+3+3+2 (9/8 + 5/8)

Group B
3+2+3+2+2+2 (10/8 + 4/8)

PART 9
Jazz Cymbal Patterns in 9/8

Section 1

9/8 is also played in groups of two and three. In this section, the student should apply the same theory learned in the 7/8 section to the groups of two and three. Even eighths are played on the cymbal while the snare drum and bass drum have a jazz triplet feel.

A few examples of each grouping will be shown. At this point, the student should further explore the possibilities already learned in the 7/8 section. Play ♪ = 152–232.

Basic Patterns

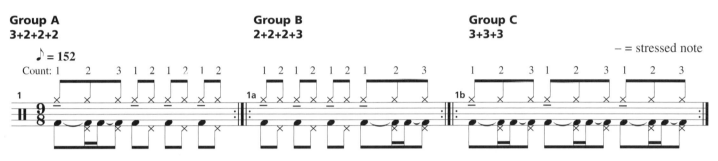

Section 2

Application to the Drumset

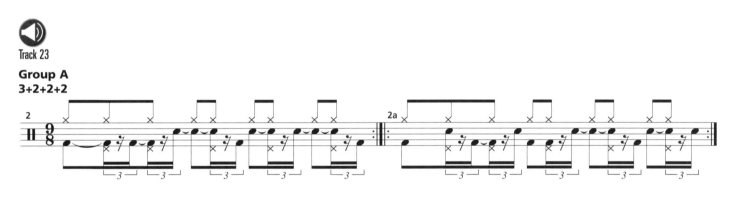

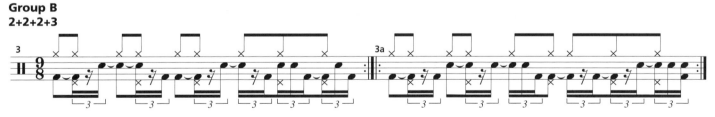

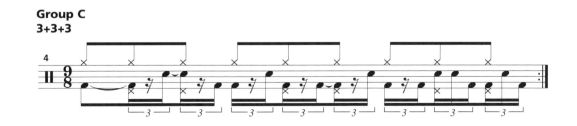

Section 3

Jazz Cymbal Patterns in 9/8

Group A
3+2+2+2

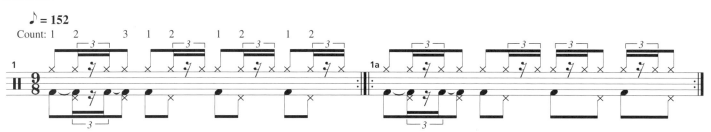

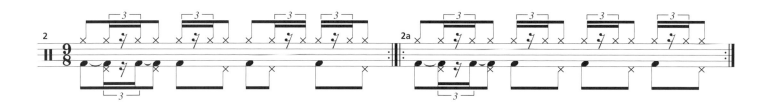

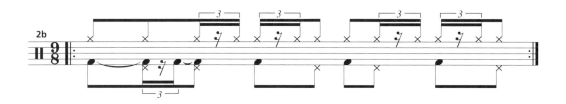

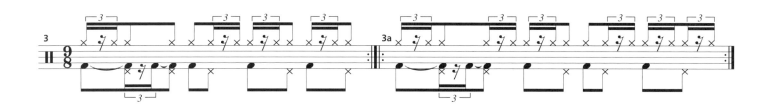

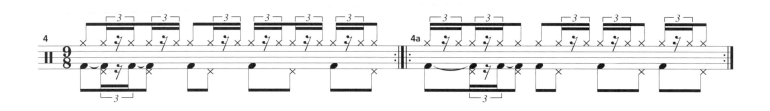

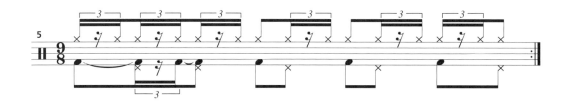

Group B
2+2+2+3

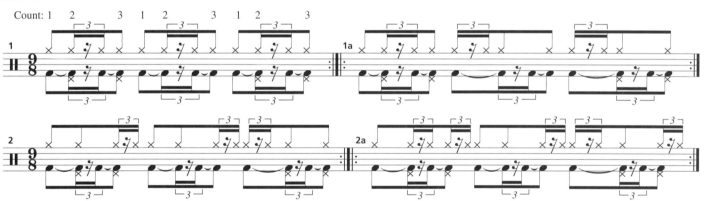

Group C
3+3+3

Section 4
Application to the Drumset

Group A
3+2+2+2

Track 24

$\quad \flat = 152\text{-}200$

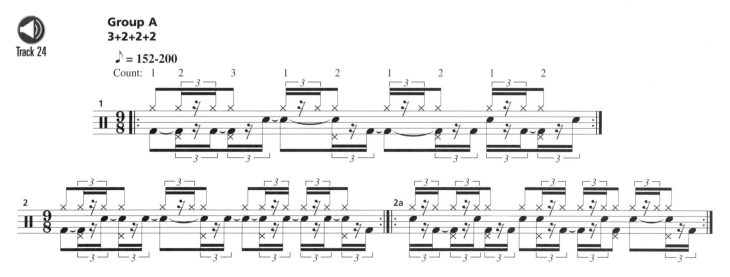

Group B
2+2+2+3

Group C
3+3+3

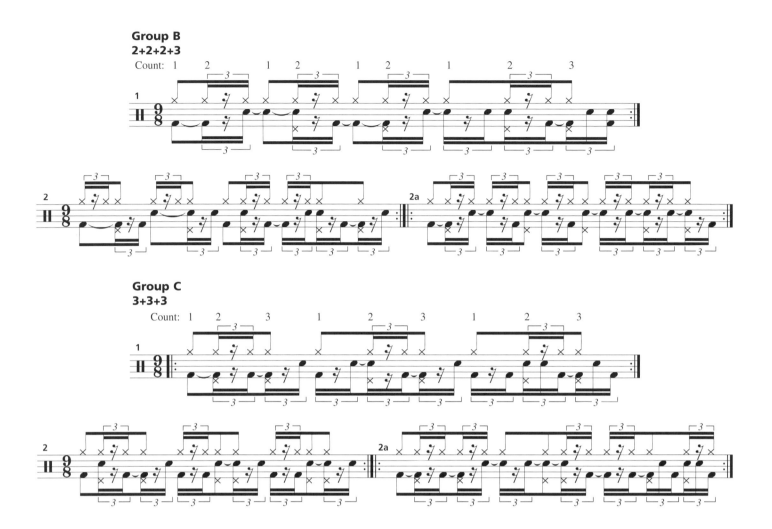

Section 5

9/8 Cymbal Patterns with Tied Notes, for Punctuating Phrases

Group A
3+2+2+2

Group B
2+2+2+3

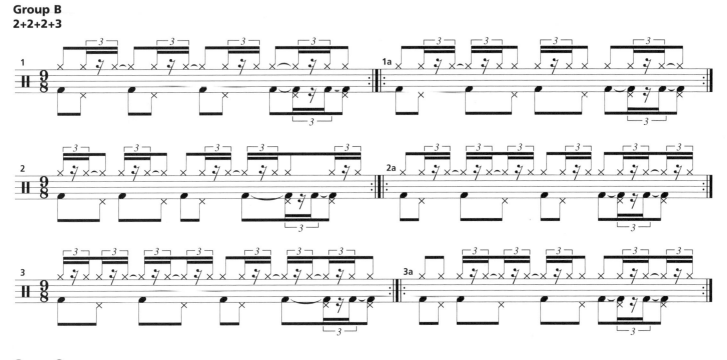

Group C
3+3+3

Section 6

Practical Application

Track 25

Group A
3+2+2+2

♪ = 152–200

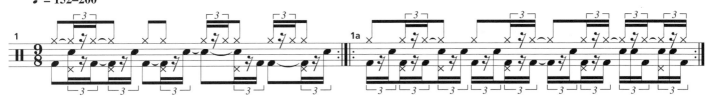

Group B
2+2+2+3

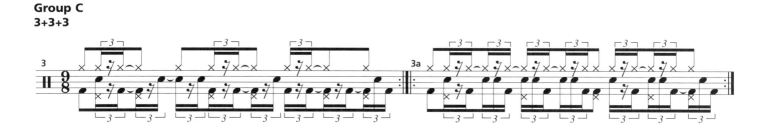

Group C
3+3+3

Section 7

One-Bar Drum Solos Developed from the Rhythms of the Jazz Cymbal Beats in 9/8

Notice that the one-bar drum solo outlines the rhythm of the cymbal pattern in these examples. Play a one-bar time-keeping pattern from section 4, group C (page 44) or section 6, group C (page 46).Group C has a 3+3+3 feel. Notice that the solos also have a 3+3+3 feel. Observe the hi-hat; it also has a 3+3+3 feel.

Track 26

Group C
3+3+3

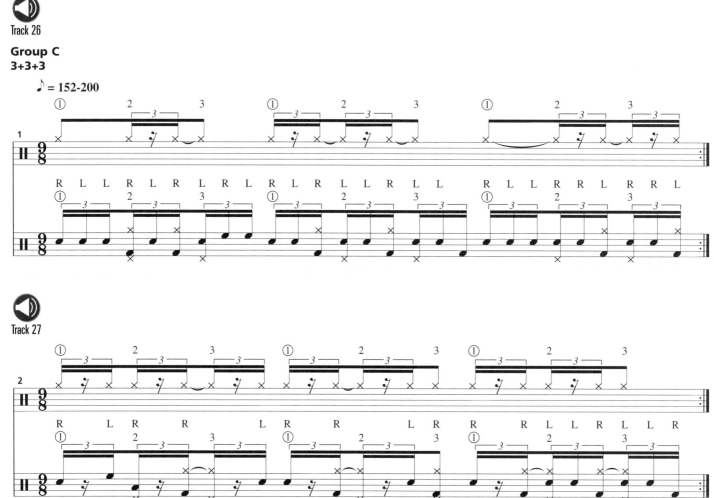

Track 27

PART 10
Developing Jazz Comping in 5/4 Time

Section 1

So that the student can become familiar with 5/4 time, the beginning of this section shows the various ways to count and feel 5/4 time.

The following examples will be played with the ride cymbal, bass drum, and hi-hat.

Group A
3+2

Group B
2+3

Group C
3+3+3+1 over Two Bars

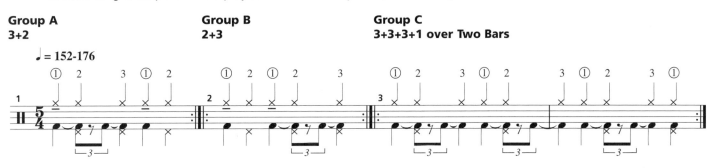

Section 2

Application to the Drumset—Basic Time Keeping

Group A
3+2

Group B
2+3 Hi-hat changes to a 2+3 feel.

Over-the-Barline Feel; Two-Bar Phrase

Track 29

Group C
3+3+3+1 over Two Bars

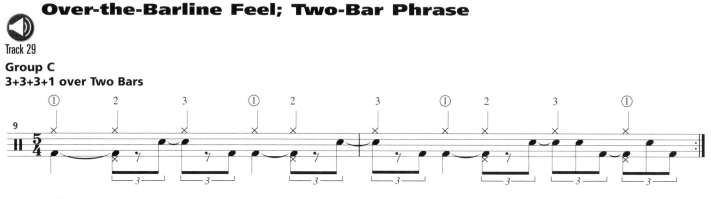

Fill Bars

Play time-keeping examples #1, #2, #3, and #4 from section 2, group A (page 47) before the following fill bars for two-bar phrases. Note: Time keeping has to have the same grouping as the fill or solo.

Group A
3+2

Track 30 Play example #5 from group B on page 47 before example #14.

Track 31

Group C
3+3+3+1 Over-the-Barline with Fills

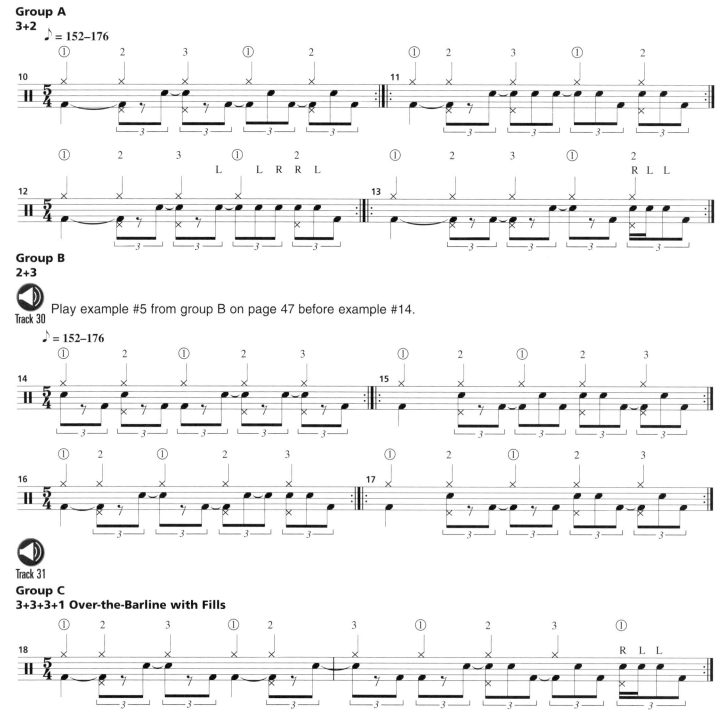

Section 3

Jazz Cymbal Patterns in 5/4 Time

The following cymbal patterns can be felt with a 3+2 or 2+3 feel. Notice that the hi-hat and bass drum dictate whether it's 3+2 or 2+3 feel. Apply each corresponding hi-hat and bass drum example to each cymbal pattern. Remember to count out loud when practicing.

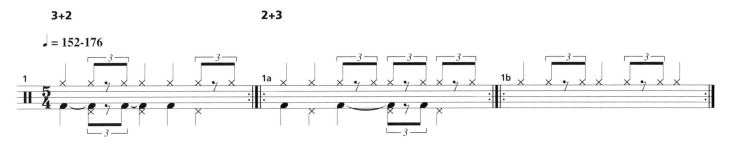

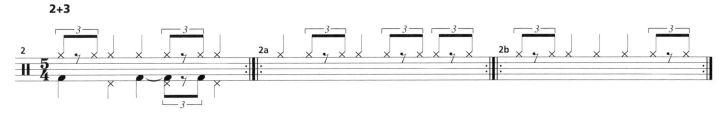

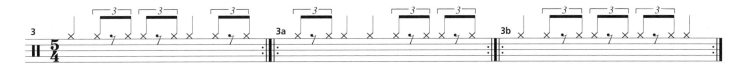

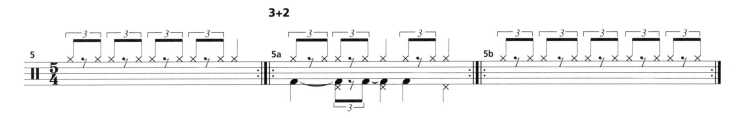

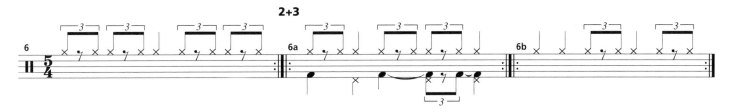

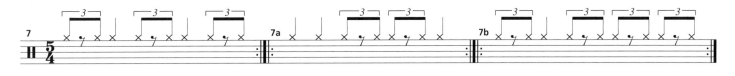

Section 4

Applying Jazz Cymbal Time for Comping in 5/4 Time

3+2

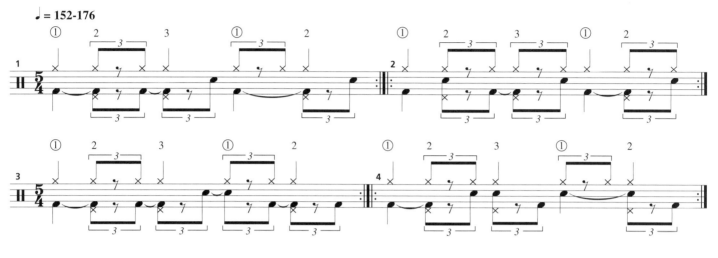

2+3

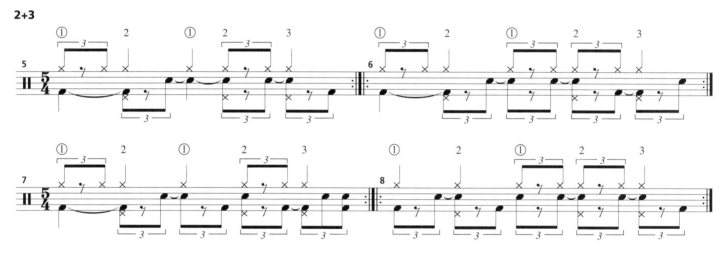

Combine examples #5 and #7 for a two-bar phrase.

Over-the-Barline Feel

Track 32

3+3+3+1

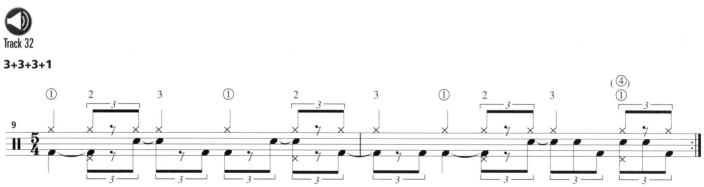

Section 5

Time-Keeping Fills in 5/4 Time

The following examples are time-keeping fills. Combine them with basic time keeping from pages 48 and 49 for two-bar phrases. The numbers in the box show the combinations. The hi-hat phrasing in the time keeping should be the same as the fill bar.

Group B
2+3   2+3

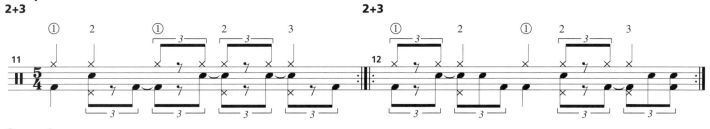

Group A
3+2   2+3

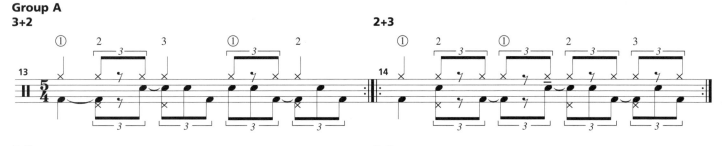

3+2   3+2

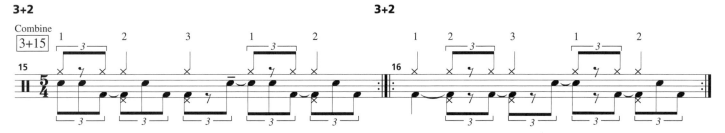

Track 33

Group B   **Group A**
2+3   3+2

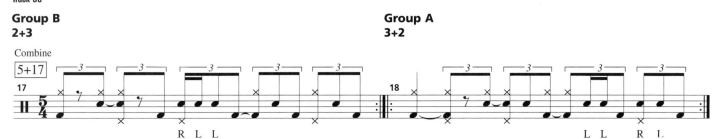

3+2   3+2

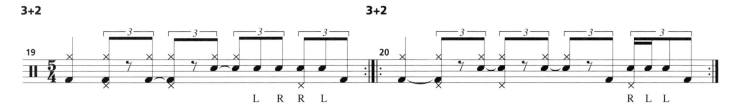

3+2

PART 11
Jazz Cymbal Patterns in 5/4
with the Use of Tied Notes

Apply the 3+2 (example 1) and 2+3 (example 7b) hi-hat and bass drum pattern to each cymbal pattern.

Section 1

Group A
3+2

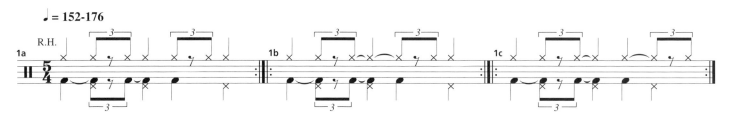

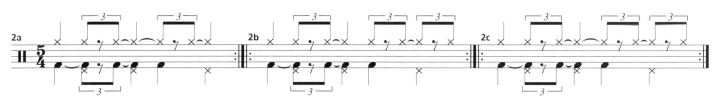

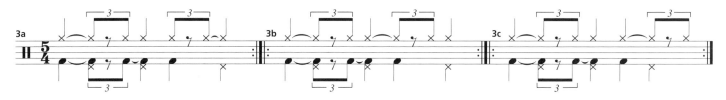

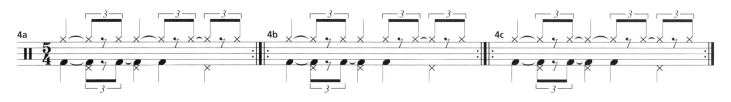

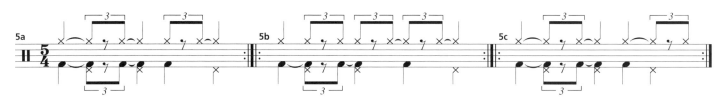

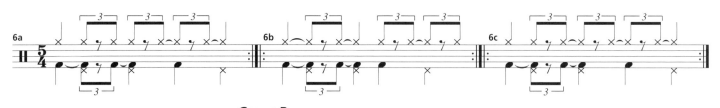

Group B
2+3

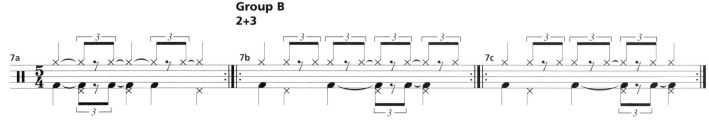

Group A

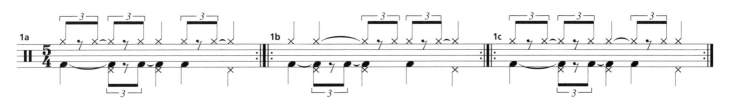

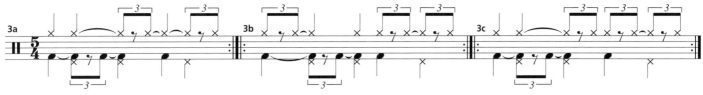

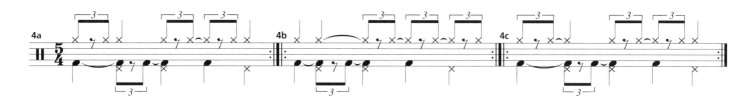

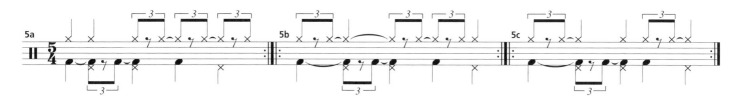

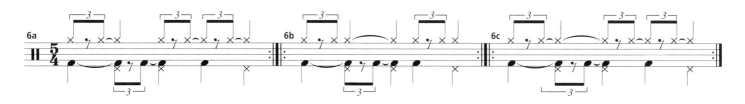

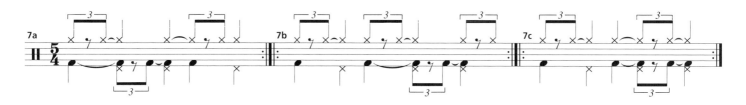

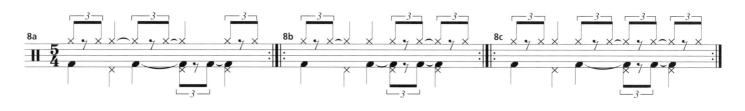

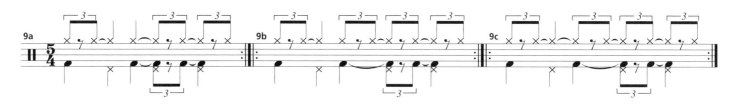

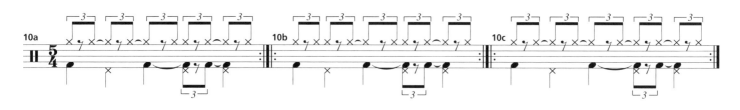

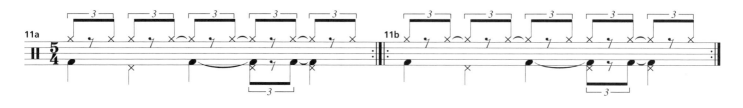

Section 2

Tied Cymbal Patterns Applied to Drumset

♩ = 152-176

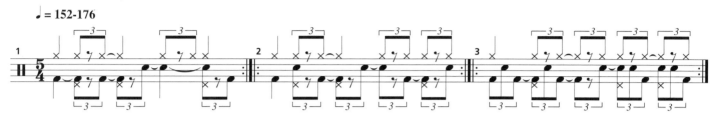

Play example #5 from page 50, section 4, before playing example #5 below.

Track 34

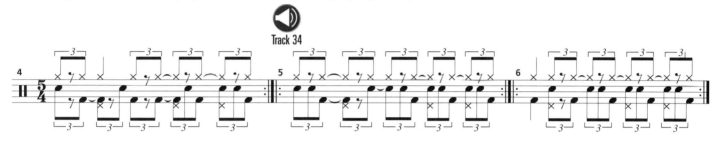

Combine example #2 with example #7. Note: This type of fill, where there is a lot of motion going on between snare and bass drum, should only be played at the last bar of a song or going into the bridge of a song.

One-bar drum fills based on the rhythms of the jazz cymbal patterns. Play example #1 before the following fills.

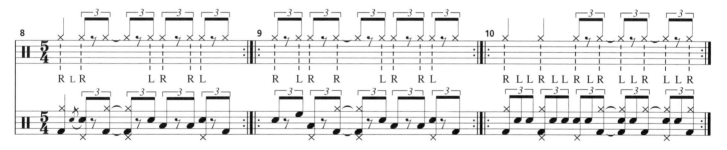

Four-Bar Phrase

Play examples #3 and #16 from section 4 (pages 48 and 49) and combine them with example #11 below for a four-bar phrase.

♩ = 132

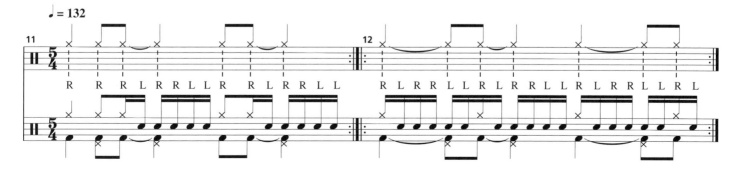

PART 12
Developing Over-the-Bar Feeling

Section 1

By making the jazz cymbal patterns into two-bar phrases, various patterns can be made to eliminate a strong feeling of one. This will produce what is known as an over the bar feeling.

Track 35

3+3+3+1

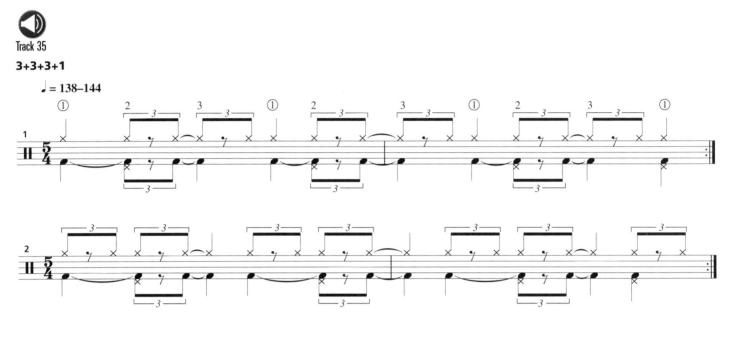

Applied to Drumset

3+3+4

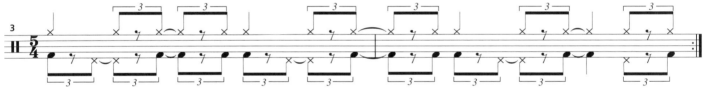

Track 36

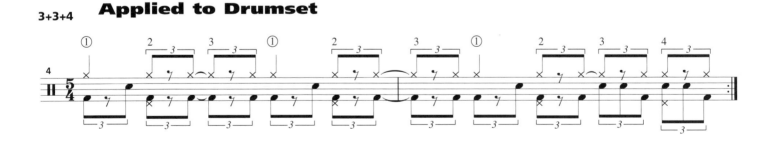

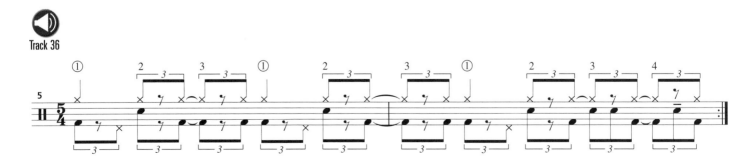

Two-Bar Drum Fills Based on the Cymbal Pattern

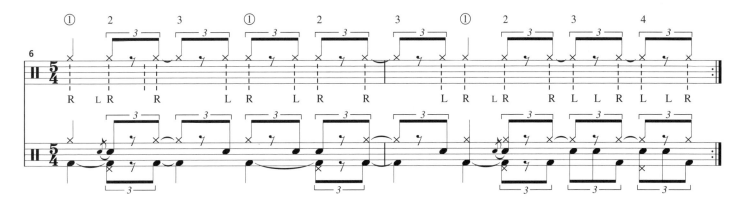

Applying the Rudiment Paradiddle-Diddle

Two bars of time in front.

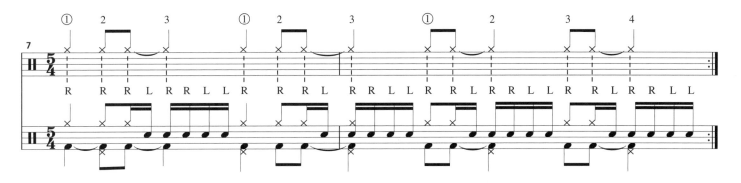

PART 13
Jazz Cymbal Patterns in 10/8

Section 1

Developing Jazz Time-Keeping Patterns in 10/8 Time and Basic Cymbal Time Keeping with Bass Drum and Hi-Hat

Group A
3+3+2+2
Counting is 1 2 3–1 2 3–1 2–1 2 :‖

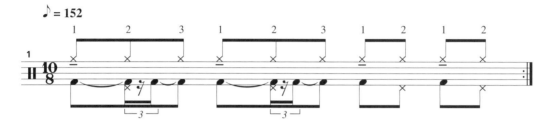

Applied to Drumset

Track 37

Basic Cymbal and Time Keeping

Group B
2+2+3+3
Counting is 1 2–1 2–1 2 3–1 2 3 :‖

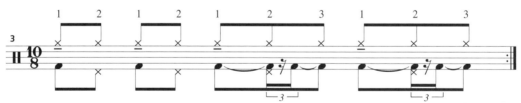

Applied to Drumset

Track 38

58

Basic Cymbal Time Keeping

Group C
2+2+2+2+2

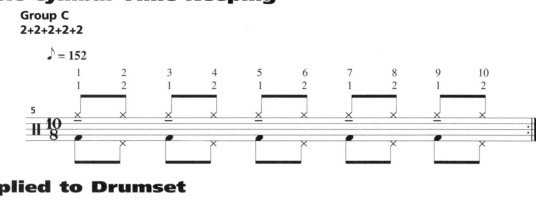

Applied to Drumset

Track 39

Basic Cymbal and Time Keeping

Group D
3+3+3+1

Counting is 1 2 3–1 2 3–1 2 3–1.

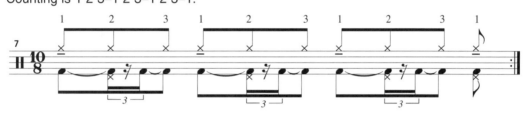

Applied to Drumset

Track 40

Section 2

Apply Jazz Cymbal Patterns in 10/8 Time

Group A
3+3+2+2

Practical Application

Track 41

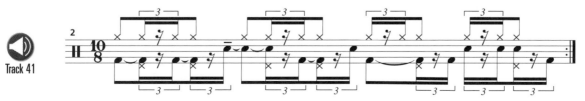

Jazz Cymbal Pattern

Group B
2+2+3+3

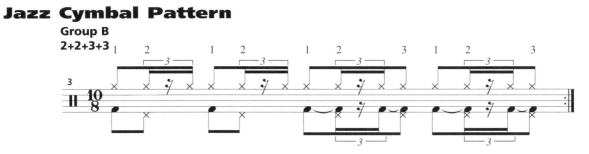

Practical Application

Jazz Cymbal Pattern

Group C
2+2+2+2+2

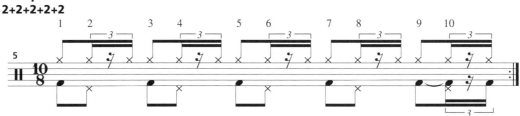

Practical Application

Jazz Cymbal Pattern

Group D
3+3+3+1

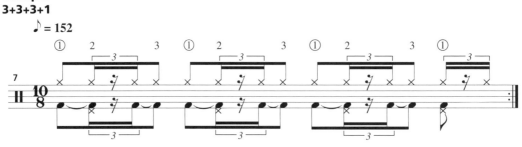

Practical Application

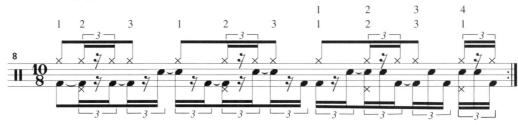

PART 14
Applying Tied Notes to Jazz Cymbal Patterns in 10/8

Section 1

Group A
3+3+2+2

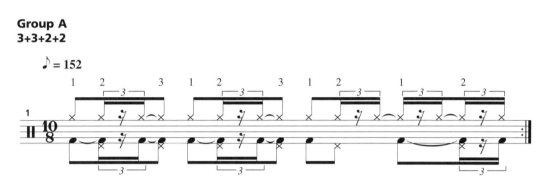

Practical Application

Track 42

Group B
2+2+3+3

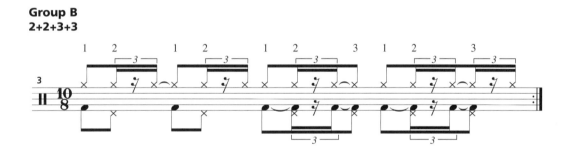

Practical Application

Group C
2+2+2+2+2

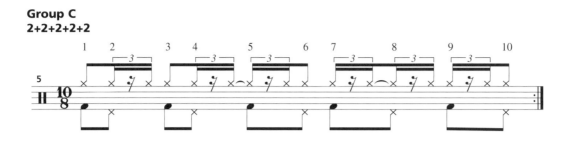

Practical Application

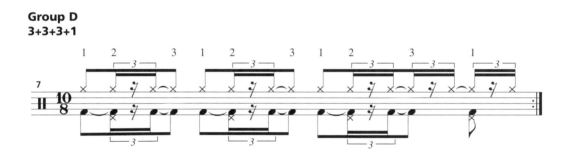

Group D
3+3+3+1

Practical Application

PART 15
One-Bar Drum Solos in 10/8 Time

Section 1

Two-bar phrase; play time pattern #2 from section 2, page 59, before the following one-bar solo. Repeat back to time pattern.

Track 43

Group A
3+3+2+2

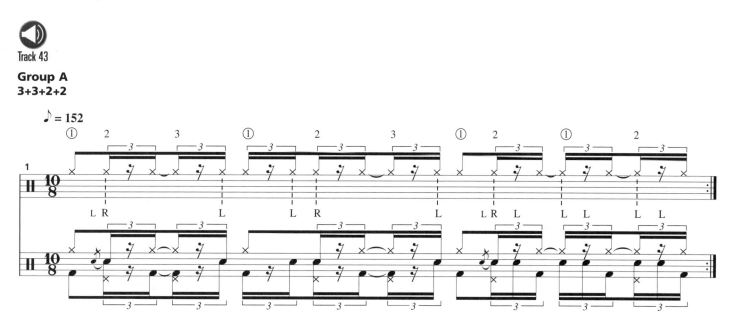

Play time pattern #8 from section #2, page 60, before the following example.

Track 44

Group D
3+3+3+1

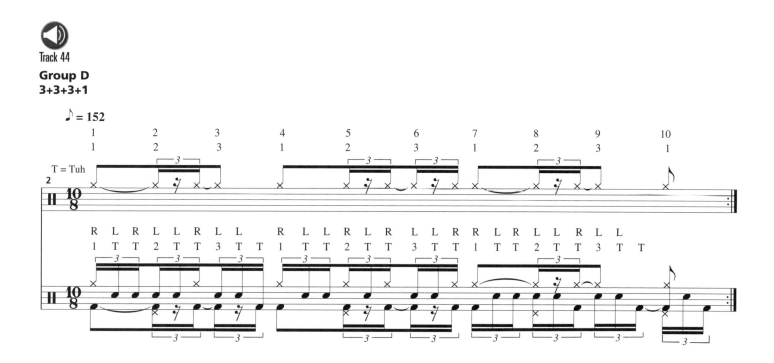

63

PART 16
Developing Jazz Time-Keeping Patterns in 11/8 Time

Section 1

Basic Cymbal Time Keeping

Group A
3+3+3+2
Counting is 1 2 3–1 2 3–1 2 3–1 2.

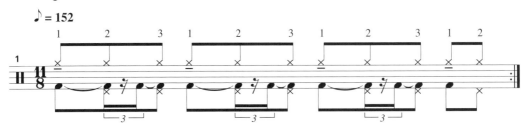

Applied to Drumset

Track 45

Basic Cymbal and Time Keeping

Group B
3+3+2+3
Counting is 1 2 3–1 2 3–1 2–1 2 3.

Applied to Drumset

Basic Cymbal and Time Keeping

Group C
3+2+3+3
Counting is 1 2 3–1 2 –1 2 3–1 2 3.

Applied to Drumset

Basic Cymbal Time Keeping

Group D
2+3+2+3+1
Counting is 1 2–1 2 3–1 2–1 2 3–1.

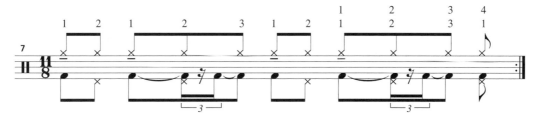

Applied to Drumset

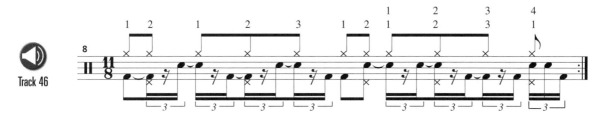

Track 46

Section 2

Apply Jazz Cymbal Patterns in 11/8 Time

Group A
3+3+3+2

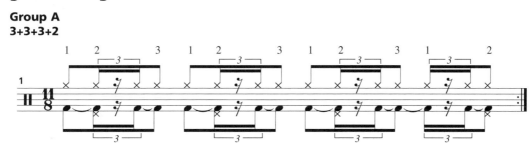

Applied to Drumset

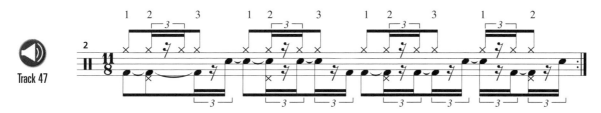

Track 47

Jazz Cymbal Pattern

Group B
3+3+2+3

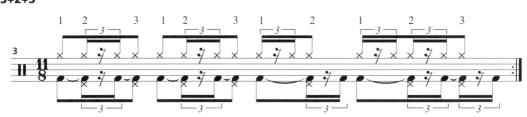

Applied to Drumset

Jazz Cymbal Pattern

Group C
3+2+3+3

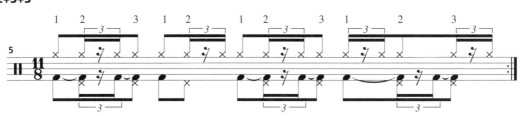

Applied to Drumset

Jazz Cymbal Pattern

Group D
2+3+2+3+1

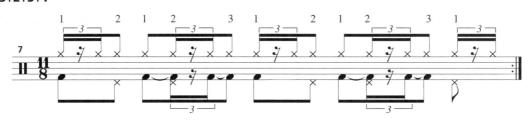

Applied to Drumset

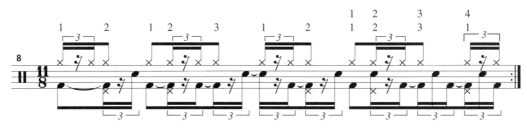

Section 3

Tied Notes in the Cymbal Patterns

Group A
3+3+3+2

Track 48

Group B
3+3+2+3

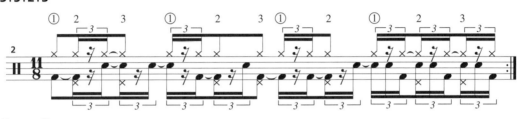

Group C
3+2+3+3

Group D
2+3+2+3+1

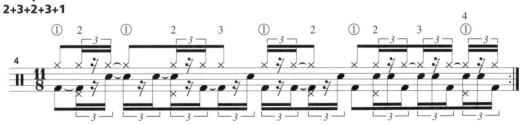

Drum Solo in 11/8

Two-bar phrase. Repeat back to time pattern.

Play time pattern #2 from section 2, page 65, before the following one-bar solo. Repeat back to the time pattern #2.

3+3+3+2

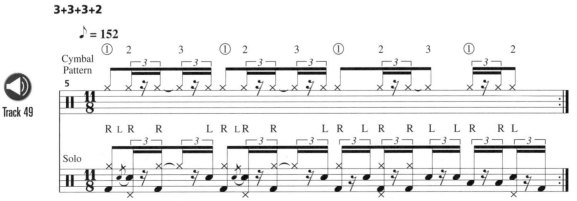

Track 49

PART 17
Developing Jazz Cymbal Time in 13/8

This lesson starts with jazz cymbal time in 13/8. Group A counting is eighth notes in 13/8:
1 2–1 2–1 2–1 2–1 2–1 2 3. Group A can also be felt as a bar of 4/4 and a bar of 5/8.

Jazz Cymbal Pattern

Group A
2+2+2+2+2+3

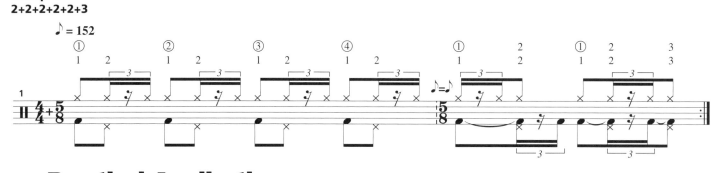

Practical Application

Track 50

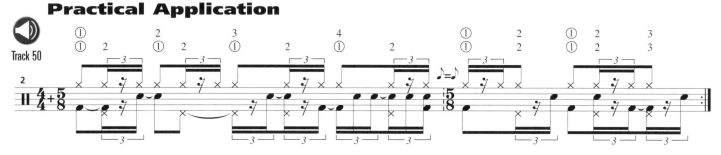

Jazz Cymbal Pattern

Group B
2+3+2+3+3

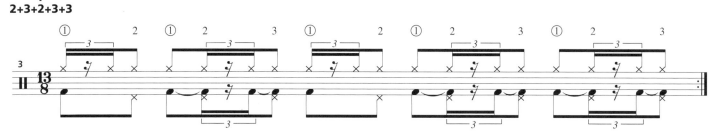

Practical Application

Track 51

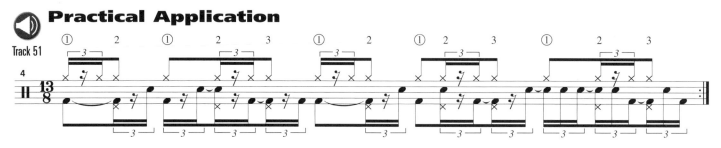

Jazz Cymbal Pattern

Group C
3+3+3+2+2

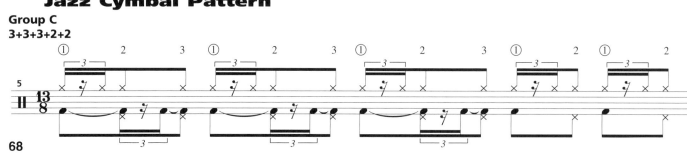

Practical Application

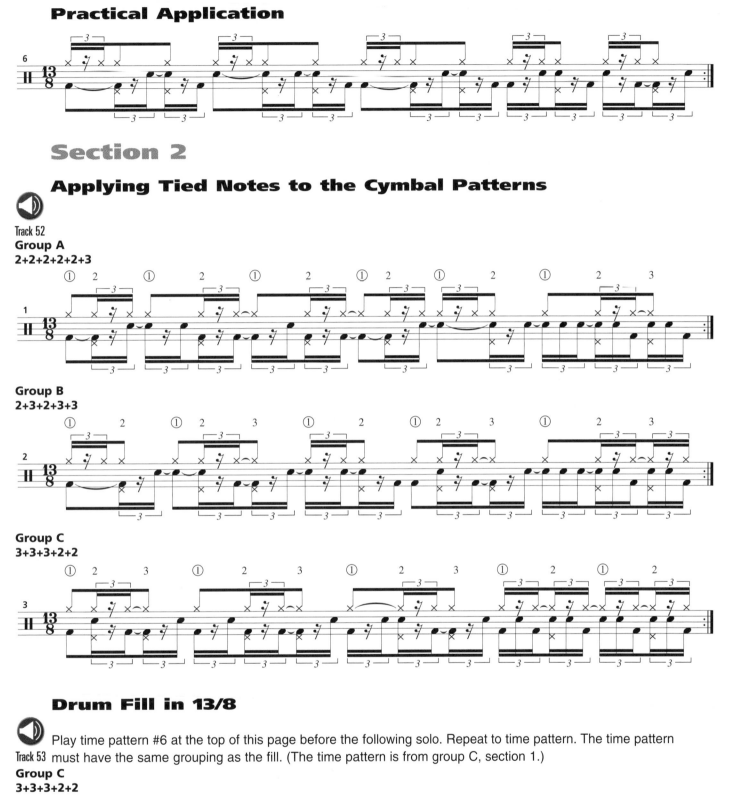

Section 2

Applying Tied Notes to the Cymbal Patterns

Track 52
Group A
2+2+2+2+2+3

Group B
2+3+2+3+3

Group C
3+3+3+2+2

Drum Fill in 13/8

Play time pattern #6 at the top of this page before the following solo. Repeat to time pattern. The time pattern must have the same grouping as the fill. (The time pattern is from group C, section 1.)

Track 53

Group C
3+3+3+2+2

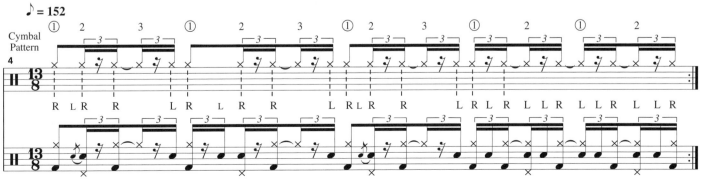

PART 18
Developing Jazz Time Keeping in 19/8

Section 1

Jazz Cymbal Pattern

Group A
3+2+3+2+3+2+2+2

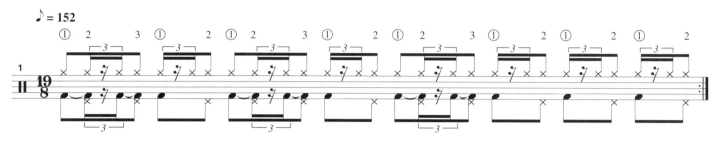

Practical Application

Track 54

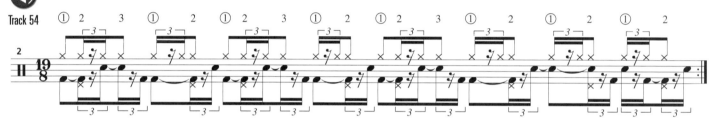

Jazz Cymbal Phrasing

Group B
3+3+2+2+3+2+2+2

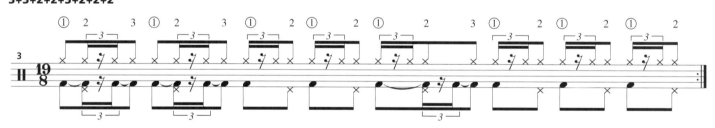

Practical Application

Track 55

Jazz Cymbal Pattern

Group C
3+2+3+2+2+2+3+2

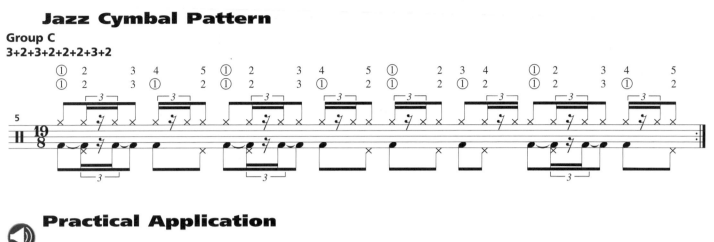

Practical Application

Track 56

Section 2

Apply Tied Notes to Cymbal Time

Track 57

Group C
3+2+3+2+2+2+3+2

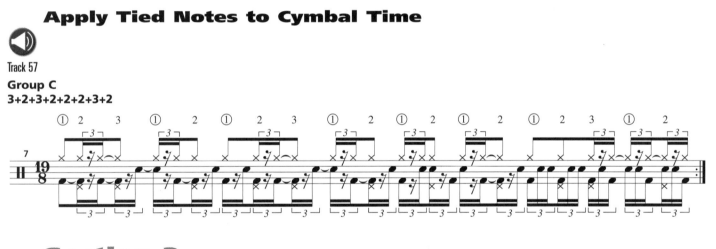

Section 3

One-Bar Solo

Play example #4, group B, from page 70 before the following example.

Track 58

Group B Phrasing Applied to a One-Bar Solo
3+3+2+2+3+2+2+2

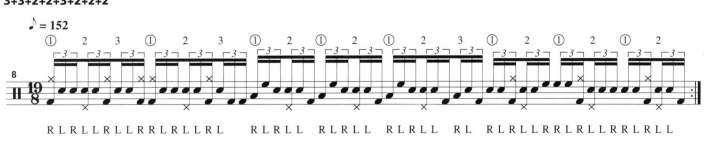

PART 19
Combining Standard Signatures with Odd Time Signatures

Section 1

In these patterns do not play eighth-note triplets in the 3/8 section. Keep a constant eighth-note feel throughout.

Track 59

Section 2

Jazz Application at the Drumset

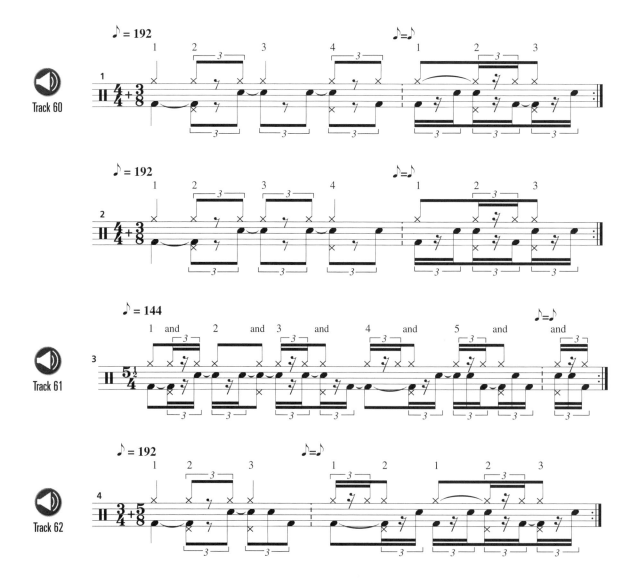

PART 20
Rock and Funk Grooves in Odd Times

Section 1

5/4 Time

In the following examples, the hi-hat plays in five. (♪) = ghost note.

Track 63

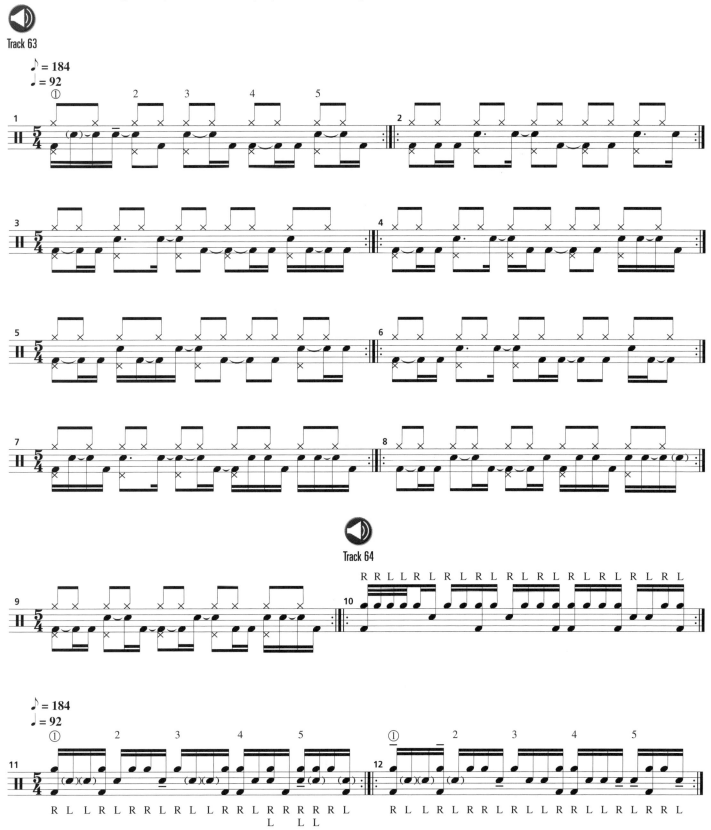

Section 2

Funk and Rock Grooves in 7/8 Time

The author stressed notes where he personally felt they should be placed. The student should experiment and develop his or her own feel for these grooves. Observe the ghost notes (♪).

Track 65
Group A
2+2+3

Track 66
Group B
3+2+2

Group A **Hi-Hat Time Keeping**
2+2+3

Group B
3+2+2

Track 67
Group A
2+2+3

Group B
3+2+2

Group A
2+2+3

Group B
3+2+2

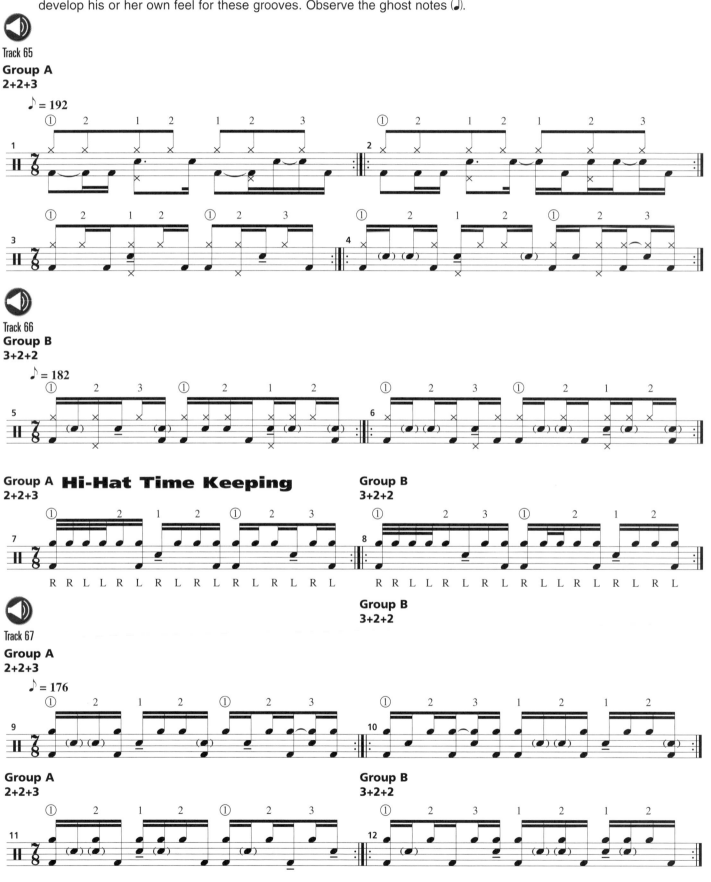

One-Bar Solo into Time Keeping

Counting is 1 2–1 2 3–1 2–1 2 3–1 2–1 2

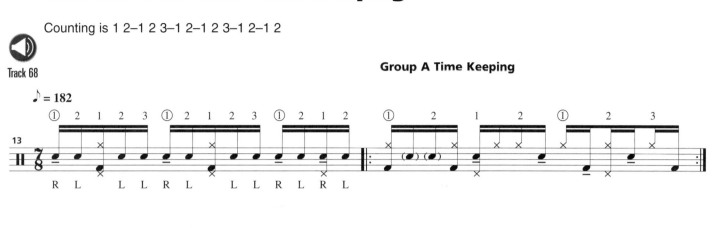

Track 68

Group A Time Keeping

Section 3

Rock, Funk Grooves in 7/4

Grouping is 4+3

Track 69

Grouping is 3+3+1

Grouping is 4+3

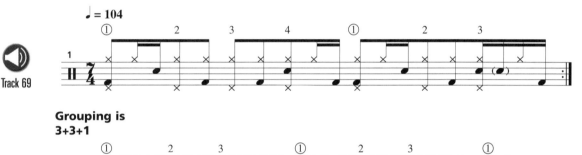

Hi-Hat Groove

Track 70

Grouping is 4+3

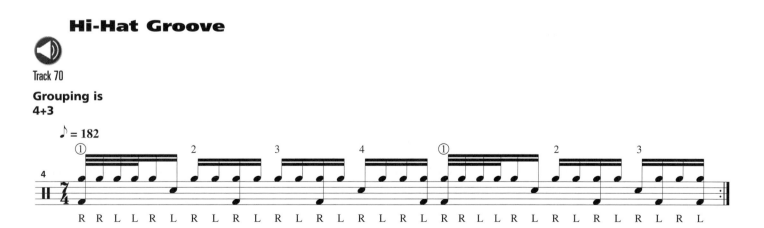

Section 4

Rock Funk Grooves with Changing Meters

Track 71

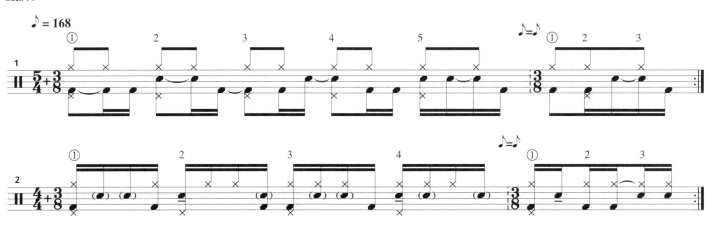

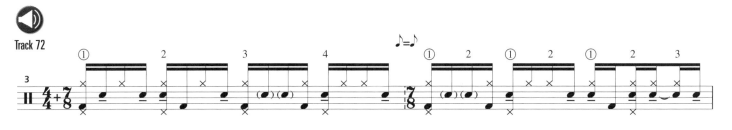

Track 72

Hi-Hat Grooves

Track 73

Linear Groove in 7/4

Two-Bar Phrase

PART 21
Latin and Afro-Cuban Patterns in Odd Times

Section 1

Latin Patterns in Practical Application to the Drumset

In these patterns, the right hand can play on the closed hi-hat or open ride cymbal. The left hand can be played with the stick across the rim of the snare drum. Combine the following examples to make up two-bar phrases (#4 with #2).

Bossa Nova/Jequibeau in 5/4

Track 74

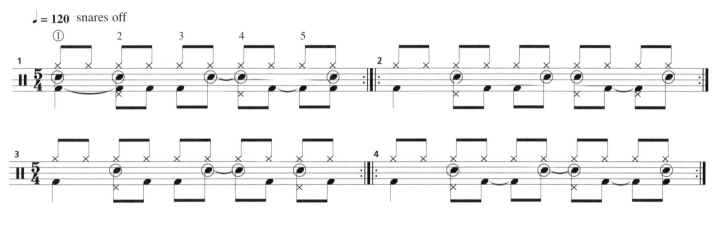

Two-Bar Phrase over the Bar Line Feel

Track 75

Section 2

Bossa Nova/Jequibeau in 7/4

Time feel is ♩ = 2+2+3

Hi-Hat Time Keeping

○ = open hi-hat   • = closed hi-hat

Hi-Hat Time-Keeping

Cymbal Time Keeping
Hi-Hat with Foot

Track 76

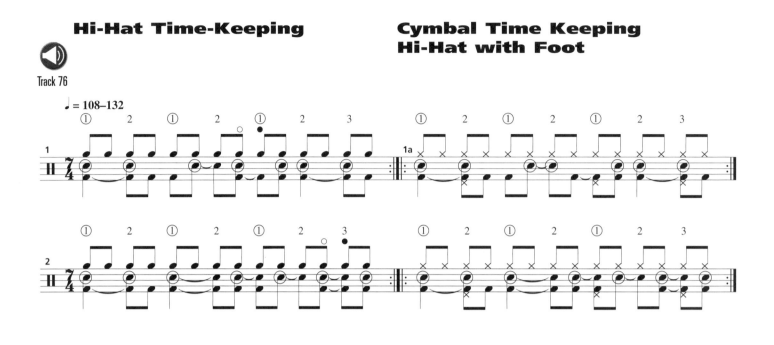

Two-Bar Over-the-Barline Feel

Track 77

Bass drum and snare drum imply the feel of over-the-barline.

In example 3, also play time on the ride cymbal. Bass drum as is. Hi-hat plays on the counts of 2-4-6 in measure one and 1-3-5-7 in measure two. The hi-hat played in this manner gives an over-the-barline feel.

Section 3

Afro-Cuban

The drumset player can approach Latin and Afro-Cuban drumming two ways. If there isn't a conga player, he can imitate conga sounds at the set. The toms and snare drum with snare off can be the open sounds of the congas. Time keeping can be done on the hi-hat.

Cha Cha

Track 78

Note: The cowbell can replace the ride cymbal.

Group A
3+2

Group B
2+3

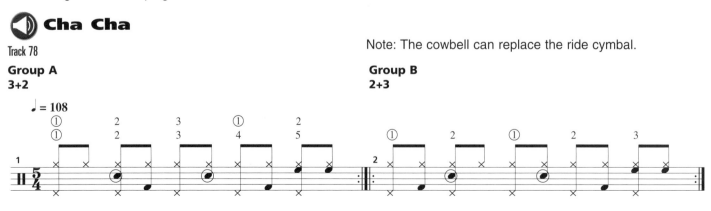

If there is a conga player, then the drummer can play the following.

The following examples are to be played when there isn't a conga player.

*omit note in parenthesis first time only

Two-Bar Phrase Combining Examples #1 and #4

Track 79

*omit note in parenthesis first time only

Two-Bar Phrase

*omit note in parenthesis first time only

Two-Bar Phrase with Conga Player

♩ = 108

Two-Bar Phrase without Conga Player

*omit note in parenthesis first time only

Open and Closed Hi-Hat

*omit note in parenthesis first time only

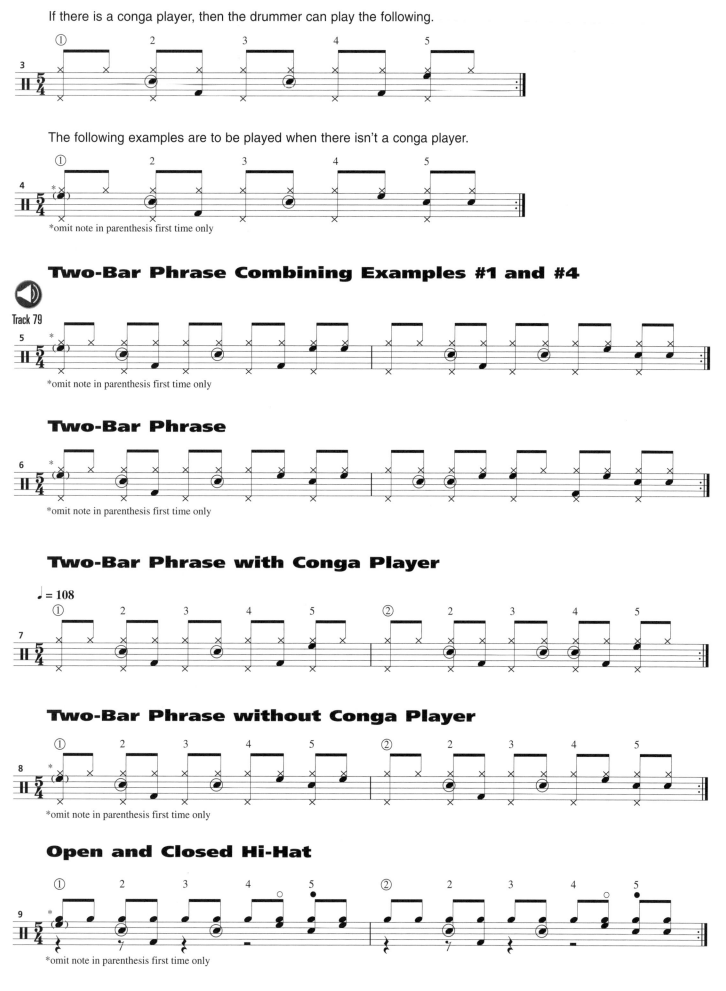

Two-Bar Phrase with Fills

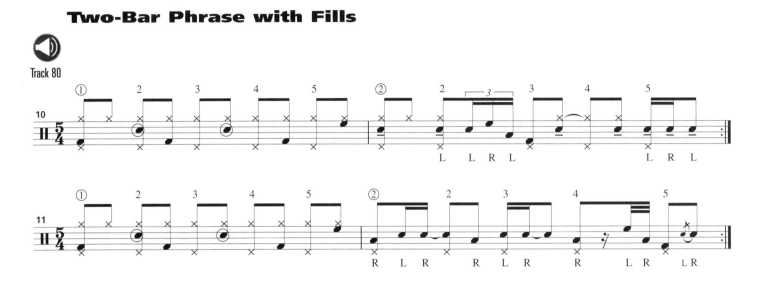

Track 80

Section 4

Mambo Patterns in 5/4

The time-keeping hand can play on the cymbal or cowbell.

3+2 Feel

Track 81

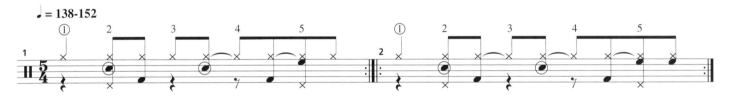

2+3 Feel

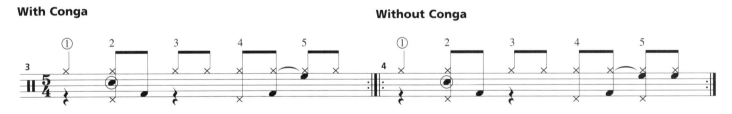

3+2 Feel Two-Bar Phrase without Conga

Hi-hat has the over-the-bar line feel.

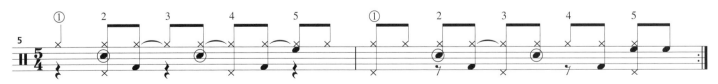

2+3/3+2 Feel

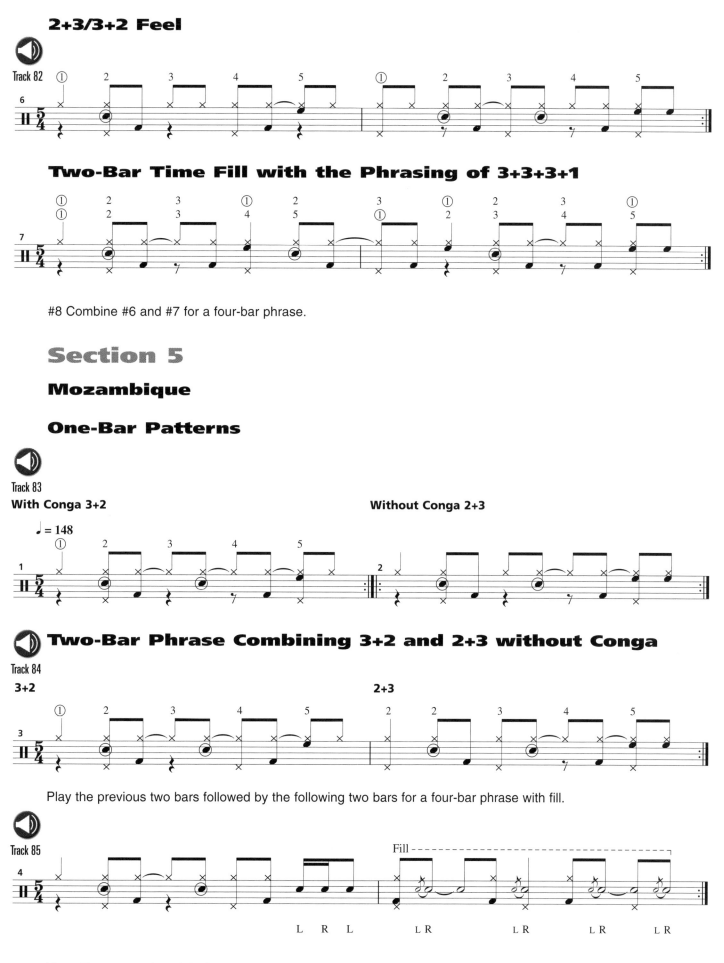

Two-Bar Time Fill with the Phrasing of 3+3+3+1

#8 Combine #6 and #7 for a four-bar phrase.

Section 5

Mozambique

One-Bar Patterns

Track 83

With Conga 3+2   **Without Conga 2+3**

♩ = 148

Two-Bar Phrase Combining 3+2 and 2+3 without Conga

Track 84

3+2   **2+3**

Play the previous two bars followed by the following two bars for a four-bar phrase with fill.

Track 85

Fill --

L R L   L   L R   L R   L R   L R

Note: To execute the stick shot in the second measure, the flam grace note should be pressed into the drum head.

Section 6

Cha Cha Grooves in 7/4

With Conga Player 2+2+3

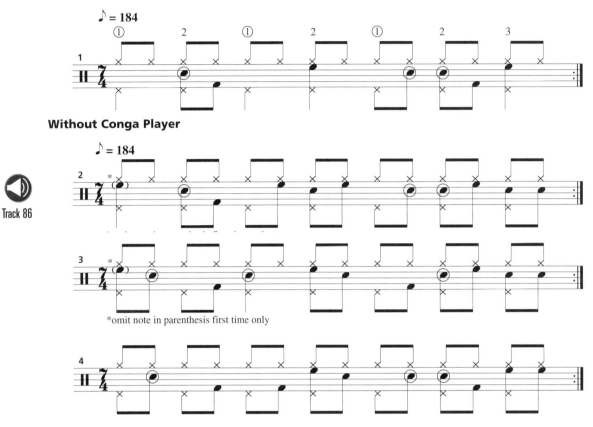

Without Conga Player

Track 86

*omit note in parenthesis first time only

Bolero without Conga

Hi-Hat Time Keeping

Track 87

*omit note in parenthesis first time only

Section 7

Mambo in 7/4

Track 88

With Conga Player 2+2+3

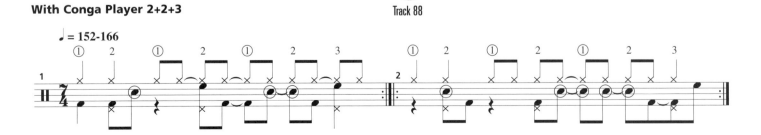

For 3+2+2 feel, start on beat 5.

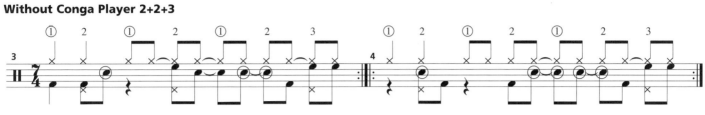

Track 89

Without Conga Player 2+2+3

Mambo Fill in 7/4

Feel is 1 2–1 2 3–1 2–1 2 3–1 2–1 2. Circled notes are a rhythmical outline for the solo.

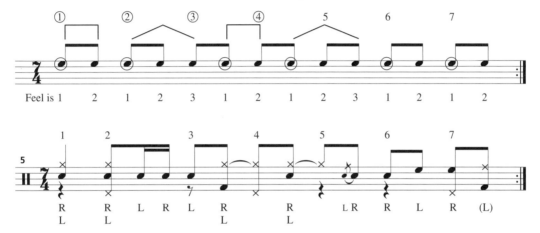

#6 Combine examples 1 and 5 for a two-bar phrase.

Additional Mambo Time Patterns in 7/4 Feel: 2+2+3 and 3+2+2

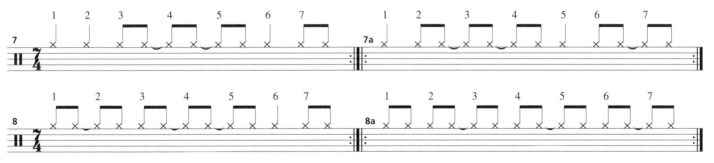

Section 8

Mozambique in 7/4

Track 90

With Conga Player 2+2+3   **3+2+2**

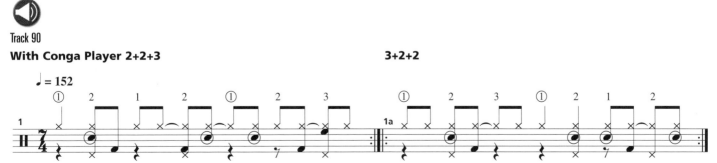

Track 91

Without Conga   **With Conga**

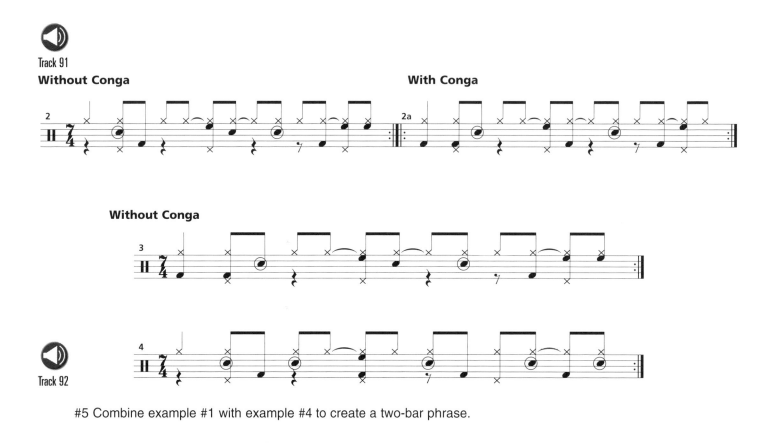

Without Conga

Track 92

#5 Combine example #1 with example #4 to create a two-bar phrase.

Section 9

Songo in 7/4 Time

Track 93

2+2+3 Feel

Same Groove without conga

*omit note in parenthesis 1st time only

Section 10

Jazz Samba in 7/8, 7/4, and 3/4

2+2+3 Feel

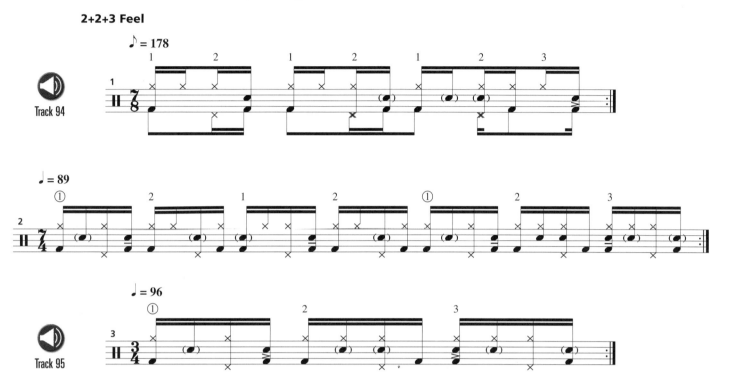

Track 94

Section 11

Traditional Samba in 5/4

The following samba grooves in 5/4 represent an early traditional style of playing samba, with one brush and one stick in the match grip manner. The brush is in the left hand and the stick in the right hand. Left-handed drummers do the opposite and also with the stickings.

Notation

The rim shot is played with the right hand about 3–4" in from the rim. The left-hand brush is resting on the head of the snare while the right hand is playing.

♩ ♩
R L = Left-hand brush is tapped with a pressing motion against the head in the middle of the snare drum.

♩
R = Right hand is played in the center of the snare drum while the left-hand brush is held against the head.

One-Bar Phrase

Track 96

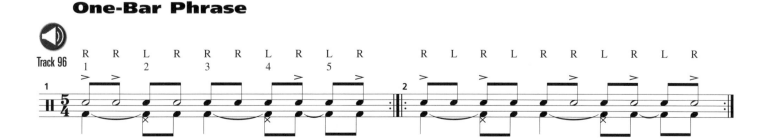

Over-the-Barline Feel
Two-Bar Phrases

Section 12

Traditional Samba in 7/4

Two-Bar Over-the-Barline Phrase